TIME, Ontology, Reality and Me

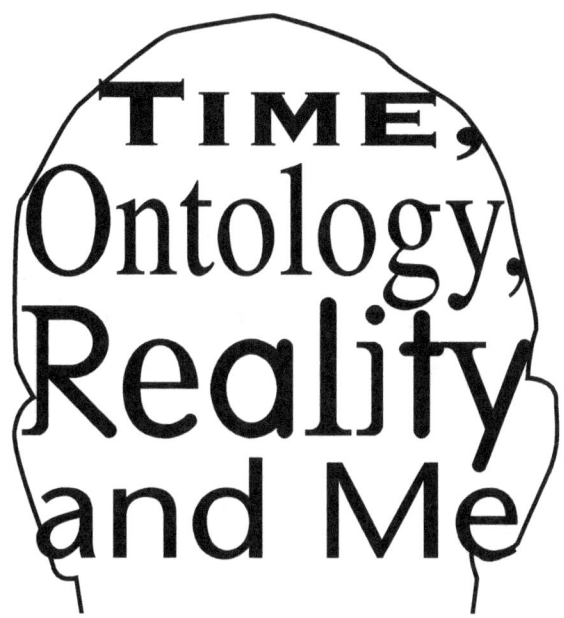

Conversations With Family & Friends

Interviewed and Compiled
by James Tantum

Time, Ontology, Reality and Me:
Conversations With Family & Friends

Published and distributed by :

James Tantum
1149 Potrero Street
San Francisco, CA   94110
jim@jamestantum.com
www.JamesTantum.com

Contents

Introduction

Having known the author many years, I approached reading his first book with a strong sense of confidence that I could grasp the many twists and turns his eclectic style was sure to throw at me.

Having known the author many years, I should have known my confidence was going to be miserably betrayed!

Having known the author many years, I received an advance copy. I was halfway through the book when, undetected by me, the pages went from one-sided copy to two-sided copy. I had been reading every other page for 15 pages. No wonder I was having trouble following the story!

Having known the author many years, I knew I had to go back and give it a re-read or I would miss an enjoyable point.

I have now completed my third read of the collection and counting. Who knows how many reads will be needed for the picture to come completely into focus? James' style is to present the reader with a completely out-of-focus story that slowly comes into focus if you are willing to keep after it, and if you do, you are rewarded with an explosion of thoughts and questions.

That's the fun for me—with each read I am provoked to ask questions. Would the same people give the same answers today? Is there difference in the answers from a generational point of view? Were current events of the time influencing any of the answers?

Perhaps you have not known the author for many years, so this is my advice to you: When you are about to throw this book out because you've read it twice and come away with one question, "Huh?" Don't give up! Give it one more read. The explosion is coming.

Roger O' Donnell

Interviewer's Introduction

I tape-recorded these interviews with family and friends in the mid-1990s and carefully transcribed them, verbatim, making sure to capture the words and spirit of what was actually said.

No editing has been done by me; I used ellipses to indicate a slight pause and "[pause]" to indicate a significant pause, a few seconds or more. I tried not to influence any answers and asked everyone to be as honest as they felt they could, considering that they were answering in my presence. I did omit some questions I asked my parents, grandmother and two others, but otherwise I believe I asked the same questions of everyone and included each question and every answer in the order I asked them. (No person I approached for this project declined.)

I am very thankful for the participants' patience, cooperation, trust and honesty. And, I apologize to them for any awkwardness they may have experienced to help complete this project. It truly could not have been possible without their participation.

I want to thank Robyn Carliss for her suggestion on how to treat "laughs" in the text, this was especially problematic for me. I also want to thank Jennifer Jett for proofreading the whole book. (I hope I made all those changes.) She also offered great punctuation suggestions, the vast majority of which I used. I want to thank Crystal Liu for her questions and observations about the things I had completely overlooked and Richard Mitchell for his helpful thoughts on typefaces. And I want to especially thank Pablo Guardiola for his insightful suggestions and observations regarding all aspects of this book. I incorporated most of his suggestions and they have truly made this book much better.

James Tantum

Who am I? If this once I were to rely on a proverb, then perhaps everything would amount to knowing whom I "haunt."
                                        - André Breton, *Nadja*

We are so accustomed to adopting a mask before others
that we end by being unable to recognize ourselves.
                                        - La Rochefoucauld, *Maxims*

There is no surer remedy for dejection than to see examples of the different virtues displayed in the characters of those around us, exhibiting themselves as plenteously as can be. Wherefore keep them ever before you.
                                        - Marcus Aurelius, *Meditations*

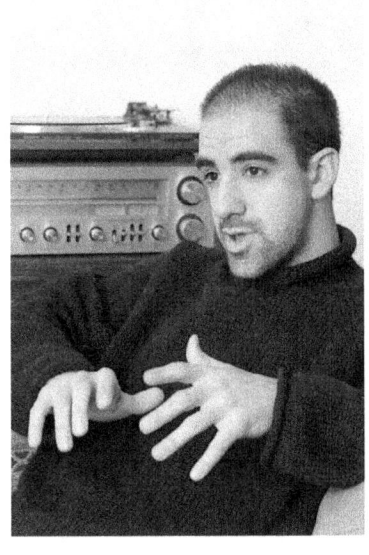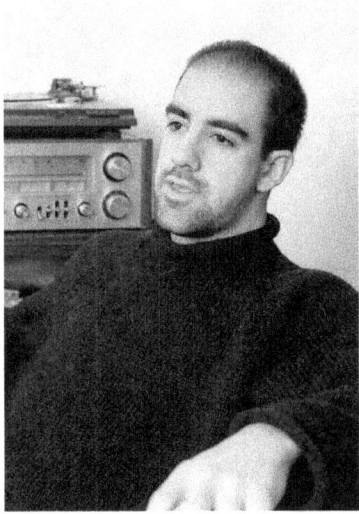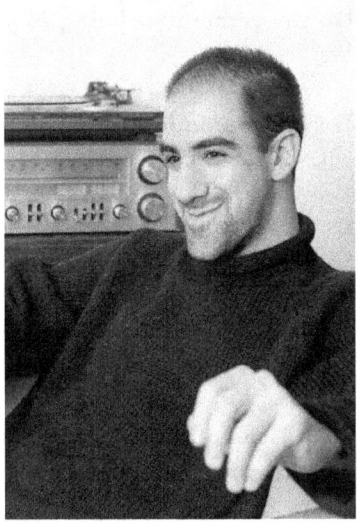

I interviewed Aram Aghazarian, my friend, in his apartment.

How long have you known me?
Uh, I've known you since...well, since I was seventeen, close to turning eighteen, and now I'm twenty-six. So probably nine years, ten years.

How much do I weigh?
[Laughs.] I have no fucking clue. [Exhalation.] You have a mysterious body weight [laughs]. You could be 150, that's how much you weigh.

What color are my eyes?
Are you going to cover your eyes now? Alright. Um, your eyes are light brown, brownish.

How tall am I?
You're five-six, five-seven.

How well do you know me?
Uh, pretty well.

Do you remember being a little kid?
Yes.

What is your earliest memory?
Um, being wheeled—I think being wheeled into a hernia operation at the hospital, which I was probably

three-ish.

Do you remember being 20 years old?
Yes.

Do you remember being 10 years old?
Uh, yes. I remember turning ten.

Do you like getting older?
Somethings I like.

Who do I most look like, my mother or my father?
I would say your mother.

Of which do I share the most characteristics?
Probably your mother.

What is your earliest memory of me?
Uh, a party for PennPIRG at Lauretta Reeves' house.

Can you name a few good qualities that I have?
[Chuckle.] No. Yeah, sure. Uh, a few good qualities, um...quirkiness, um...sense of humor, playfulness... your clothes [laughs], you know, the stuff you wear.

Can you name a few bad qualities or weaknesses that I have?
Hmm, inability to...to share certain personal information...that I need for my files [laughs]. Bad qualities. Well, sometimes you won't say what you are feeling; uh, hiding anger, I would say. It's usually—it can often be very good—it's good to have that ability but if you are angry I don't think you express it. Instead you channel it somewhere else. You get a back log of...and uh...also you store away too many things in your apartment. That's a thing you do, it's your pack rat quality. Um, [exhalation] you have a bad habit of collecting things and then giving them to people as presents when they're just things from the trash, like a, you know, an oversized map of Delaware mounted on [laughs] Styrofoam that doesn't even fit in my house and that I have to throw out [laughs], like, the next day [laughs]. Let's see, I'm going on a lot longer about the bad qualities but, uh...bad qualities? Not much else outstanding.

What in general are great qualities to have?
Definitely a sense of humor and uh, sincerity. Qualities just in general, as a human being?

Yes.
Optimism, unpredictability, spontaneity.

Who do you admire or find inspirational?
Who do I admire or find inspirational? Certain teachers I have had. My biology teacher in high school, Dr. Stamper, uh, I guess. Certain athletes: Eric Heiden, people like him. My parents.

Are people at base good or bad?
People are horrible at base; people at base are base...But occasionally some people are good at base, like me and my friends.

What are my hobbies?
Your hobbies? Hmm...putting together things [chuckle] that happen to be in your apartment. Your hobbies are various art projects, uh...going to museums, um, I guess bike riding, is that a hobby of ours? It's just a thing we do. Is a hobby something you take—can you take a hobby seriously?

Yes.
Thinking about sex...that's just a commitment [laughs] that's barely a hobby, that's just a commitment. What the fuck hobbies do you have, Jim? What the hell do you do? I have no idea. You, uh...I don't know, talking on the phone [laughs], Xeroxing things. I would say, I don't know if this is a hobby, but record keeping, um, documentation of everything that you've done or seen [laughs]. Everything that has passed in front of those eyes there's probably a notation somewhere. I don't know if that's a hobby either, that might just be some kind of problem [laughs], you know, some kind of a tax thing, life deduction.

Who are some of my close friends?
Me, uh, myself, probably Aram would be one of your close friends. Uh, Don, definitely Jack, Sherone, you know, basically guys [chuckle]. Who else is a close friend or yours? Jackie, there's a girl. Some guy named Roger. Yeah, those people. Who else is your friend? Who else do I get together with? Or do I hear about you talking to on the phone? Hmm...I feel like I'm leaving another person out that I see a lot. Maybe I'm not. Oh yeah, Darryl Funchess. We'll leave it at that.

What are some of my favorite things?
Your favorite things, um...one of your favorite things is...analyzing your friends' problems and having very good counter examples as a way to connect. You love doing that. You like analyzing things. Talking about Art, talking about movies. [Laughs.] You like getting—well, I don't know if it's one of your favorite things, but well, you know, your projects, your, uh, things you make in a shop and mount pictures on. Definitely. Your, uh, hall of fame, anything that you've made go under your favorite things. Was that the question, what are your favorite things?

Yes.
Um, you know, I think probably your friends and women, which are not friends [laughs]...spiking all your guests' drinks with Galliano...Bush's Baked Beans.

What are some of your favorite things?

[Laughs.] Never mind, I don't want to incriminate myself. Some of my favorite things? Definitely my friends, my close circle of friends. Riding my bike...that probably sums it up. I don't have any other specific favorite things. I could go on for hours though if you want me to talk about it.

A few more things might be nice.

[Laughs.] You know, um, getting rid of all the dust bunnies on my floor. Um, watering my plant. Oh, eating, eating. Eating, that's a big one. Eating is major. Eating yogurt, eating spinach, Italian, Japanese, um...my mom's food. That's one of my favorite things. Taking home food my mom has made and not saving for the week but eating it all in one sitting [laughs]. Late night pizza. And also, B-rated soft porn on cable, that would have to be up there.

Who is the most famous person you've met?

Uh, Carrie Fischer, I would say. Um, yeah, I don't think anyone comes close to that; I can't think of anyone. Um, no. Then Jack Frederick following.

How many people are alive in the world?

How may people are alive, in the world? What spiritually or just like pulse? [Laughs.] Somewhere around five billion.

Are you convinced of God's existence?

No, I'm not convinced. No, I occasionally call on him, it, her or hook but I'm not necessarily convinced.

Do you think you have free will?

Sure, to some degree, yes.

How do you deal with that?

How do I deal with that? Um...I deal with that—well, I must deal with it on a subconscious level because, uh...because I probably don't think about my "free will" in this way too often. Um, but I would say how I deal with it is...is just by sitting down and having a sandwich and relaxing.

How many ideas of how to live, or what life is about, are your own?

How many ideas? I don't know. There are probably maybe a couple, uh, I mean I have no idea where I get some of my ideas from. I don't know where the hell they are now, that's for sure. I don't know, how could they not be somehow a composite of all the things you've heard coming from other people?

Do you remember a time when I wasn't around?

Uh, no; I mean all through my adolescence and childhood there was [laughs] just sort of this presence. So I'd have to say no, I don't. When I met you it was just like, "OK, here he is finally." You know, but you were always somehow there.

Aram Aghazarian

Can you name 3 very important events in my life?

No [chuckle]. Um, I would say, well, I would say graduation was probably important to you. That was probably an important event. I wasn't there for you, but—or was I? When did you fucking...well, whatever [laughs]. I would say graduation was important. Important things in your life. I don't know, that's pretty difficult. Um, to think about it as an event-based thing or maybe, you know, for whatever—I wasn't sort of present for whatever epiphanies you've had over the years, um, you know. I don't know, I mean I've been with you, I guess, when you've done things that you were pretty proud of, which might be good for the sort of highlight reel, but I don't know where they fit in your sort of most important list.

[Exhalation.] The, uh—I don't know what the two other most important things would be because I don't know you—well, I don't know you before the age of twenty-four or twenty-two, before you were twenty-two...you know. I don't know if it's necessarily a job promotion that you've gotten or a, you know, or just riding your bike in -20 degrees to Levittown, or, uh, you know, there seem to be a number of things you are, like, happy that you've accomplished. I don't know if they—I don't feel like they are monumental enough to belong in those three spaces. Oh, and your trip to Europe.

What most explains why I am like I am?

Um...Levittown, your parents...and the presence of electromagnetic fields, the availability of triple E widths in shoes [chuckle]...wide you are [chuckle]. Um, I don't know. I would say it has a lot to do with your parents. I don't know them very well but...your dad—probably tailgate parties at Eagles games have a lot to with...what explains you as far as you via your father. I know how you describe him. You don't talk about your mother too much, as far as what she's like. But it's things like, as a personality, your dad seems to be...like I can see—he seems kind of aggressive like, you know, "What the fuck" type of guy. I know why you lay back, you lay back and go, "Hmm, I don't know," sort of a cautious, sort of an analytical, um, but, uh, I would say Levittown is a biggie.

Do I look different from when you first met me?

As opposed to when I last met you? You—yes, you do look different. Your, well, I don't know what your hair was like then. Um, you, I don't know, your skin is a little bit different. You look older, Jim. Your hair, I don't know if your hair was short or long; I think it was long. See, now you've gone back to that, like, crazy, [chuckle] lunatic, unpredictable-looking hair that you had around that time, I think. Your hair was generally kept a lot longer as far as I remember. But, you know, you look like an older man, you look like, in fact, the older man in my life. Uh, actually you've weathered pretty well over the last 19 years, or however long it was, from 22 to 30, that would be eight. You look pretty much the same.

What is the dumbest thing I've done?

[Laughs.] Um, wow, the dumbest thing you've done. [Laughs.] I don't know, probably, like, at Ruth's Chris Steak House, like, putting your, uh, like, last morsel of that fine steak that you had into your broccoli soup and asked it to be put into your doggie bag, uh [laughs]. That was probably, I mean that was sort of insane, I don't know how stupid—if it was stupid, I mean because she shouldn't have, like, arranged your doggie bag for you in front of you. But to conceal a piece of meat in soup at a fine restaurant is pretty dumb [laughs]. Uh, I don't know, what other dumb stuff have you done? Dumb? Um, I don't know, that stands out for me.

Can you name 3 very important events in your life?

Um, well, my bike accident...would be one. Probably, uh, well, graduation was pretty important, from high school and from college. Those were pretty important...because, like, I just couldn't believe I got through it. I don't know, climbing Mount Katahdin with my father which is—I wonder how old I was? I was—my dad was in his mid 50s so I was probably like 16 or so. Winning the 60 meter dash in the all-elementary school olympics...and, uh, those are some standouts.

What most explains why you are like you are?

What explains why...I don't know, if I knew the answer to that, um...we'd be dealing with each other on a totally different level [laughs]. If I knew the answer to that, put it this way, we wouldn't be friends, [laughs] this interview would not be taking place. What that explains why I am, not what explains what sort of epitomizes me, but what explains? Hmm...brother. I mean, I have to bring my parents in for that, sit them down and—I have to—you should, I guess, come to my house, look in through the window, like, you know, how you would look in as an observer in a special booth like when you're watching surgery through special glass, you can watch over the operating room. You could see me in action at home and, you know, we wouldn't know you were there. I would say it is my family and probably, you would have to take some lab samples, and stuff like that, and then throw those results into the mix as well, because I'm sure that has a lot to do with it. I don't know what samples [chuckle] we're talking about here. Let's leave it at that.

What would I consider some of my favorite places?

Um, the nape of my neck. Uh, some wall that you scaled that there is a picture of you in, [laughs] that wall is probably one of your favorite places. Um...hmm...probably the art museum is one of your favorite places and, uh...probably between the thighs, why should I leave that out? Who could deny it?

What are some of your favorite places?

Hmm...the mountains in southern France where my cousins live; um...the pond, the lake that our cottage is on in Maine; um, slums in north Philadelphia, abandoned factory areas and breweries; definitely north Philadelphia. In fact, the area along Second Street in north Philly. And, uh, the barber shop.

When was I probably most depressed?

Um, after you and Sue broke up for a time. You got back together after, but at some point you broke up and, um, I got together with you at a World War I monument [chuckle], or was it, uh...it was in Washington Square park, near the eternal flame, near the Olympic torch. I think you were the most depressed I have ever seen you then.

When was I probably most excited?

When, well, it was excitement but with—excitement and fear probably when, uh—oh my God! I knew I left something out, your trip to Europe. That was a big one, I think. And you were pretty excited although you were scared and immediately [laughs], you know, just downplaying what Europe could be like: "It's going to be like America. Yeaah, I'm going to go to Europe." That type of thing. But I think you were pretty excited. Yeah, that's it.

When were you most depressed?

Most depressed. Probably...when I took out a plastic ruler from my pencil box and—never mind [chuckle]. Well, I think I was depressed when Andrea and I broke up, like, in 1991, or two, 1992. I was pretty depressed. It has always been breakups, I think, when I felt the most down. [Exhalation.] Yeah, I can't imagine, like, feeling more beat than that...for a long time. And also when my friend died when I was in high school.

When were you most excited?

Probably when I was in Rome in '91—90! "I bid $90 for that washer and dryer." [Laughs.]

What would I consider my greatest achievements?

Didn't you ask that already, Jim? [Laughs.]

No.

Um, what would you consider, not what I consider your greatest achievements. You—what would you consider your greatest achievements? Hmm...I don't know, you have been traveling with, like, World Game and stuff like that. I think you ran—I don't know about that. You've run a workshop on your own, right? When you travelled somewhere and no one, whatever, someone didn't meet you because their plane went down or something [chuckle], that's horrible. Um, yeah, I remember you were pretty proud of that, although you weren't as proud, like, as when you were saying "I did it," when you went to Europe the first time, and last time. No, that's not true, you've been there since. You seemed more—you felt like you really accomplished something, "Goddamn it, I did it! I did that." So, uh, that again...accomplishments?

I don't know, is it done, is the *Hairpiece* done? OK, sorry I asked. [Laughs.] When that's done that *could be* your greatest accomplishment because it's just going to be—all hell is going to break loose, like the fucking Hindenburg blowing up, that's going to be like...but that doesn't count because that hasn't happened yet.

Um...I don't know, a single accomplishment. I think it is going to be graduation again, from college. It just seems like, I don't know what else you compare to that. I would say when you were on the honor roll in college specifically, I think you were very proud of that. Weren't you in, uh, you had some academic achievement going on there. It was before I—I don't think I was even in high school yet but—[laughs].

I need a third. Probably, uh, I don't know, wasn't there something really, really big that you ate in one sitting? Was it that time we had, like, 12 desserts? That was major [laughs]. That probably doesn't count. I don't know if it was a bike thing, if when you went to Pittsburgh with Jack, you know, and gave me the finger from 500 miles away and thought you were something, and you thought that was a big achievement, of course that was made up for by the Vermeer exhibit [laughs], gung ho and fucking no show [chuckle].

Achievement. I have no fucking idea about achievement. I think, uh, I mean I keep thinking on terms of like achievement, award, a plaque or whatever, you know. The funny thing is you collect things that are about achievement that aren't yours, you know, trophies, uh, you know, that type of stuff. It's kind of interesting. Achievement. Probably, I don't know, it's probably like an eight-hour phone conversation; you like, you didn't hang up with one of your friends for, like, eight hours. It could have been me, Sherone, Jack, David Serline—is it Serling?—[chuckle] Rod Serling. I don't know, it could be, like, a personal achievement; I shouldn't think in terms of, like, things that were handed to you. I just have no idea of what you consider as an accomplishment, Jim. I think you're accomplished as far as, if you view it that way, as far as your friends. But I don't...I don't know if I want to pursue that.

What would I consider my biggest regrets?
Biggest regrets. Hmm. [Pause.] I think that, uh—I don't think of any specific regrets, like I wish I had, you know, asked that girl out on the spot or something like that. But, um, but I think there are a lot of times in your life where you had opportunities to seize upon that, you know, I guess rationally speaking, there is no reason not to do. Like there are so many things to get done, so many things you want to do. And you're more active now as far as, like, when you want to do something you're more likely to do it in a short amount of time, and more focused.

I would say that you regret, you know, your dilly-dallying or delay for whatever the cause, doing what you want, getting done, whether it's your trophy case or getting a job in the right place. Because we have gotten together many times and have made endless lists of shit we had to do and then never actually follow through; and uh, I would say not following through on things, or getting started on things earlier, um, are the basis for regrets.

What are your greatest achievements?
Greatest achievements. I don't know, my first thought is really on, probably on an interpersonal level. I mean I feel very proud of my friends, my buddies. I mean, I don't know, I don't necessarily consider that—I don't know that I consider that an achievement but as far as things that are, you know, in a great deal caused by me, you know, having a lot of friends, I'm very proud of that. And the kinds of friends that I have. I mean, I don't like to think about it this way, but I feel like, you know, around me, or and around that I have sort of engineered a great group of people that I'm very proud of. So I suppose you can consider that an achievement.

I don't know, I have difficulty like, you know, especially being a non-achiever all through school, although—well, that's not entirely true, at least not in college. Um, I don't know, I mean I don't think about my achievements as like photography or all my activities. I really don't think of those things in terms of achievements, or at least I don't consider them that way. I think that, um, I don't know, I guess I don't feel that I've had many achievements in, like, photography, at least not achievements. I've made good photographs. I've, well, uh, I guess my *New York Times* photograph, that, that'll classify—thank God I came up with an achievement, Jesus Christ. Um, you know, that was really good. I'm very proud of that actually. It's the only thing that keeps me going [laughs].

But I mean, like, as far as all my other activities, like, all the things I'm involved in, involved with, I just like, well, achievement? Well, I'm doing something at it. I hope to achieve things in them but, uh, you know, there are little things that I'm proud of. I guess achievements is such a big word that it has this

Aram Aghazarian

connotation where, you know, where anything you did, that you're proud of, doesn't measure up to what "achievement" is. An achievement would be, like, discovering, whatever, a new vaccine or a, you know, that takes care of some horrible disease or something. But, you know, like, I'm proud of certain rides I've done, like a 100 mile very difficult ride up in Maine that I did. Even just you and me, like, training and doing the [Manayunk] Wall competition. It was something we decided we were going to do, we trained for it, and we did it, and we did very well given the amount of, you know, training we put in. So...we'll put achievements to rest for now until we accumulate some more.

What are your biggest regrets?
I think, uh, well, I don't know. I probably should have gone to the military. The older I get the more I think, "Hey, if I went to the fucking army that would have gotten me in shape." I would have gotten done a lot more because it just would have taught me, sort of, better, more efficient ways to harness, you know, the skills that I have and, sort of, maybe give me more strong direction, greater structure and discipline. I wish that either—my parents didn't want to send me to military at all, but I kind of wish they had done something like that because, uh, I don't think it wouldn't change—would I be a photographer or whatever "-er," whatever the things are I do that, you know, all together plus "e-r." I don't know if I would still be that, do those things: guitar, writing stuff, experiment with acting thing. I don't know if I would do that.

But hmm, I regret like [exhalation] sort of—but I had no control over it—regret putting myself in a situation where, you know—although work for Bill Cramer was like boot camp, though. I don't know how much that—it has affected me a lot. It's like, I almost had to travel a certain distance in order to get to where I am. So it's, like, in some ways I look back and it's, like, well, can you regret it? Or is that the way it had to be: It could only have been that way? It's probably not alright to look at it that way either. You do have choices, but I wasn't ready to make certain choices then, so, and they could not have been made, unless someone else made them for me. I don't know if that makes any sense but that's about it.

What is some of my favorite music?
Your favorite music? Jimmy's? Uh, well, 2 Live Crew [laughs] or you might want to erase that part if people are going to see the transcript. Oh, B-52s, Woody Allen soundtrack: the *Manhattan* soundtrack, Dave Brubeck. You like all sorts of shit, you know, '70s albums of all sorts, um, you know, *Shaft, Shaft* album, um, certainly. Hmm, well, you like certain big bands, big horn sound, at least in the way we've distilled it in our musical pursuits. What other music do you like? I don't know. You like music with good drums; you think you'd be a drummer if you were some kind of musician. But, uh, so maybe you can assemble a drum kit based on things you find in the trash. Maybe in 10 years you'll have a complete set.

Can you name some of my dreams or goals?
I don't know about your dreams, well, at least not dreams you've told me about that you had at night. Your goals? Probably to crush everyone at some point, to smush them like fucking aluminum cans.

Your goals. I don't know what they are; I can only speculate. Isn't it funny that I've known you this long and I don't know what your fucking goals are? "What are your goals and dreams?" It's like you ask me that now and I'm like, "I don't know this guy." And I just, like, listed having a good rapport with, like, a good group of people as one of my achievements. Well, obviously, now you know the truth to that.

It's a fucking fraud. You may as well not buy anything I say for the rest of this tape [laughs]. But uh, I'd think you'd like to exhibit things you do, like to maybe—I don't know if you'd want to sell these projects you do, like *Hairpiece* and stuff like that, but I think you'd love to have a show at some point, or you'd like to be in a position to profess—not that you don't do that now—but I feel like something in the Art world...

Your goal is to be somehow seen, to communicate, to show yourself. I don't think all these things—all these little projects you do are simply intended for your room on Spruce Street. So, uh, I think your goal is to be a follow-through man, get stuff done, does what he says he is going to do, and likes doing what he says he is going to do...kick ass.

What are the most important things one can get out of living?

Food, oxygen, all the amenities. Um, what's the question? [Laughs.] What are the basic things, what are the best things? Well, that living is amazing and that...um, I mean, what do you want me to say, as opposed to what? What's the best you can get out of dying? Wh—what are some of the most important things one can get out of living? You mean what is important in life? [Laughs.] See, if you don't ask the question right, then I'm going to take it literally and do some like rhetorical son of a...professor, like, analysis of the question and criticize it.

I think, uh, that one of the best things you can get out of living [exhalation], bastard...good time, a good experience, feeling like you did something worthwhile, or that you did the right things for yourself... and understanding the value of your time while you are living, not at the last moment...What else? A new car, a convertible...year supply of Minwax, a racing bike, and, uh, a good open place to ride.

Is working an evil necessity?

Yes. Pretty much, at least I think so. I don't know [laughs]. When I don't work I start to feel like a piece of shit, *but* on the other hand, well, what do you mean by work? Work for money...if I get done stuff I'm supposed to do like writing stuff, photographing, the important stuff, um, then I feel good. But that only just prolongs things cause if I don't make money, it doesn't matter, I'll move back home to my parents so I won't meet the rent and I won't eat [exhalation]. So, yes, it's an evil necessity; it's a pain in the ass.

Is it hard to be happy in life?

Is it hard to be happy in life? Unfortunately, I think for many people it is. I mean, there are a lot of things that I should be happy for, happy about, and I am when I think about it, but I don't think about it enough. I just dwell on the negative stuff way too much and, you know, it's just—and that's for a person like me, I'm in good shape, you know, I'm relatively—I'm healthy, my head's above water, you know, I'm involved in stuff I like to do so I should be happy, but yet—and I should readily say, "Yeah, I'm happy." But, um, but yet it is a challenge to be happy.

I envy people who are just happy no matter what their condition. And I have met people like that, you know, they have a pretty bright spirit. And there are other people I see, like, that should not be, I mean should definitely be happy for what they have but are not because they've got something rotten, you know, there's some problem at the core. So, so it should not—it should be easier to be happy but actually I think for a lot of people, and myself included, I have to [exhalation] to remind myself, I don't know, it just —I don't know.

Aram Aghazarian

A lot of times it is hard to be happy, happy as opposed to neutral and living, you know. It's not either, like, happy or not happy, it's like, well, it's almost like, well, why be neutral? It's unfortunate just to be neutral, sitting there like, "uhhhhh," and not knowing what the fuck is happening. It's hard. I'm learning to be more happy more often, less neutral less often, and less unhappy more often. But it just seems like it takes a lifetime for some people, which is unfortunate. A lot of times I can say to myself, "OK, shit, let's shift modes right now. Whatever you're doing, just fucking cut it out. Stop being a baby and just go, are you alright?" and almost, like, will yourself to a better state of mind. 'Cause there's a lot of stupid stuff that you should not be unhappy about. So, I guess based on all this blabbering, I've pretty much said it is; it can be very difficult to be happy.

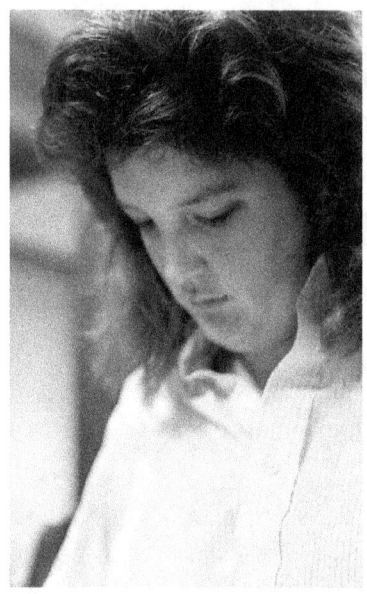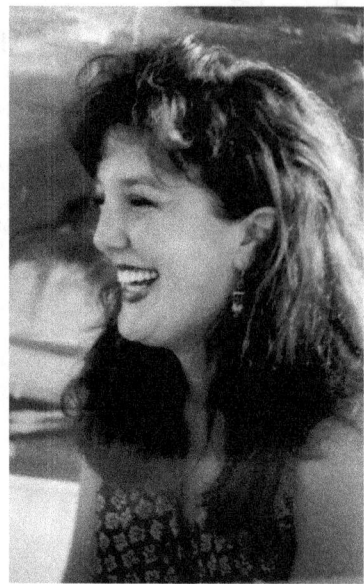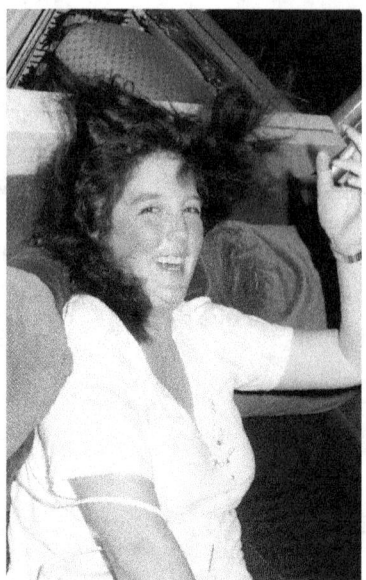

I interviewed Theresa Collington, my friend and ex-roommate, over the telephone. I asked her to think in terms of the last time she saw me to answer these questions. (Photographs are from that time period.)

How long have you known me?
Um, since 1987, so in 1995 that would have been 8 years.

How much do I weigh?
I knew this was going to be like this [chuckle], 170 pounds.

What color are my eyes?
Hazely-brown color.

How tall am I?
About five foot seven.

How well do you know me?
On a scale of one to ten probably, I would say, uh, given the time frame that we are talking, probably, probably, uh, 8 maybe even a 9.

Do you remember being a little kid?
Yes.

What is your earliest memory?
Sitting in the corner, in a diaper, pulling a raw waffle out of the toaster and eating it, facing the corner, in my parents' first apartment.

How old were you?
How old was I? Pre one-year.

Really?
Yes.

Do you remember being 20 years old?
Yeah.

Do you remember being 10 years old?
Oh, yeah.

Do you like getting older?
Um, yes and no.

If you want to be more specific at any time you can be but I am not going to press that.
Well, yes because, you know, the things that, definitely, wisdom seems to accrue exponentially as you get older. But, no, because realities of life become more visible to you with that wisdom and it can sometimes be painful.

Who do I most look like, my mother or my father?
Your father.

Of which do I share the most characteristics?
Your mother.

What is your earliest memory of me?
You?

Yes.
I remember—my earliest memory of you was being in the office at the Program Board and you and Danielle Sciocchetti and I were having a conversation and you, I don't know, you were sleep derived or something—but you were talking about toilets and you were cracking yourself up, and you could not stop laughing and you were like, "Imagine if people just rode toilets through the street or you put toilets in your living room as furniture and people were expected to sit on them." And it actually was very, very funny and you got us both to the point where we were both cracking up like two lunatics.

I do remember that actually.
And the fuel sticker.

Can you name a few good qualities that I have?
About you?

Yes.
Yeah. [Exhalation.] Um, very smart; very intellectual; uh, very eccentric and will stick to your eccentricities even though your friends might really bust your chops and give you a hard time; um, you've always been able to surround yourself with very cool people; um, you're a tremendous, tremendous friend; a great listener; um, a fun roommate; a dependable roommate; a dependable person; um, always interesting, never boring, God knows. And, uh, you have a good sense of what is fair and what isn't fair and you and I always seem to have the same kind of, like, um, sense of justice.

Can you name a few bad qualities or weaknesses that I have?
Um, [exhalation] I have—I have to think about that for a minute but I don't know if I have to pause. Um, I think you sell yourself short…I think that in some situations you were, um, not as confident as you could have been in your own abilities. Um, I don't necessarily consider this a bad quality, but maybe—it was something that I was always kind of, um, envious of—you sometimes could be very introverted…One of the good qualities I forgot is that you are good at keeping in touch with people, the bad thing is that sometimes we don't hear from you for years [laughs]. I think that's it for bad stuff, and that's a stretch.

What in general are great qualities to have?
In a person?

Yes.
Just the general—general great qualities that a person could have?

Yeah.
[Exhalation.] A good heart; integrity; benevolent; um, unselfishness; kindness; um, a sense of humor, a good sense of humor; an intelligent sense of humor, not at the cost of others; um, an appreciation for the arts; an appreciation for the simple things in life; um, God, uh, um, a sense of empathy for people around them, um, in good situations and in bad; someone that protec—protectiveness, people that are protective of their family and friends; um, intelligence but without abusing intelligence [chuckle]; um, generosity; um, I guess that's it.

Who do you admire or find inspirational?
Um, that's a hard question right now in my life, that's wh—why I have been kind of looking for. I admire my husband, um, because he's super bright and super humble. Um, I don't really admire anybody I work with. Um, I admire my brother, Chuck, because he's genuine and, uh, he's able to achieve—find great happiness in the simple things in life.

Theresa Collington

Um, famous-people-wise, this might sound queer, but I admire the singer Sheryl Crow. I think she's really cool and I think she has a cool lifestyle. And I like—um, I admire the woman that wrote the *Murphy Brown* [television] series, Diane Ford, I think her name was, um, cause she didn't do it until she was 42. Um, I admire my dad's mother a lot cause she had nine kids and she loved every single one of them very intensely, very good, very kind, very nurturing person. Um, who else do I admire? That's about it.

Are people at base good or bad?
Good.

What are my hobbies?
Jesus Christ, I don't have all day. Your hobbies are: you like to read; you like to listen to music, back in '95 I think you were still on vinyl; um, you like to collect things, you like to do projects; um, what else, read, collect things, do projects. Um, you've always been kind of like a city dweller, I kind of consider that kind of a hobby; um, you like to take pictures; um, what else, um, hobbies for Jim. Mainly I remember the collection—collecting things; um, taking one man's garbage and turning it into art seemed to be a big thing you liked to do; um, people watching…and definitely reading, I think that is all I can remember.

Who are some of my close friends?
Uh, Aram, um, Sherone, Sue, me, Tamra Feldman; um, I think you had a friend named Phil, you had a friend named Jackie growing up; um, who else [exhalation], Deb, that we mentioned earlier, Deb Schroeder I think her name was, Deb Shrader. Uh, closest friends, like your inner circle, I mainly remember Aram and Sherone; um, Don, the guy we used to call Book Man.

Um, who else? Who else do I remember as your friends? I think that is about—oh, you were friends with Danielle Sciocchetti too, um, and Alissa, when we were friends in college. I don't know if I would consider them as close friends, as the ones I mentioned before; um, Sue Lerch. That is all that I remember. Oh, and Miriam Koffler.

What are some of my favorite things?
[Chuckle.] Oatmeal. Uh, you mean possessions that you have or things that you like, like to do?

Uh, it is pretty wide open.
OK. Some of your favorite things: um, your books; your things that you have collected over the years; uh, your projects that you have done; um, you're not a guy—you're not a very materialistic guy so your list of favorite things would be minimal. Cats, cats are one of your favorite things. They count. Um, you didn't really seem to ever really have a lot. You just, you uh…um, I wouldn't know what your favorite food was, um, but I probably could think of it if I tried. Basically, probably, I would say your books and the things that you collected, the things over the years, like your Cootie Bug collection and your refrigerator door things and your, um, you know, just the things you keep on display in your home.

What are some of your favorite things?
Some of my favorite things? Music, um, the beach, my books, uh, some particular books that I have, um, most importantly, my memories. That's about it.

Who is the most famous person you've met?
God, Madonna. I met Madonna but it doesn't really count because I didn't really talk to her. Um, God, I met a lot. Most famous person I've met? Gene Simmons of KISS.

How many people are alive in the world?
Two hundred and fifty billion [chuckle].

Are you convinced of God's existence?
No.

Do you think you have free will?
Yes.

How do you deal with that?
Carefully. By making decisions as carefully as I can to make sure that they have the best effect on me and the people around me.

How many ideas of how to live, or what life is about, are your own?
How many ideas of how to live, or what life is about, are my own?

Yes.
I would definitely say most or all of them. I mean as far as how I'm living, most of them are mine, I'm not like—I'm not like anybody else that I know.

Do you remember a time when I wasn't around?
You?

Yes.
Yeah, before I met you.

Can you name 3 very important events in my life?
Uh, sure, sure. Um, let's see, losing your virginity, graduating college and your relationship/break up with Sue Lerch.

What most explains why I am like I am?
[Laughs.] Um, I don't know, you're definitely a mystery.

Theresa Collington

Do I look different from when you first met me?
No.

What is the dumbest thing I've done?
[Laughs.] The dumbest thing you've done is fall without wearing a bike helmet in the middle of Center City [Philadelphia] on the foot traffic, rush hour, while wearing green goggles in the middle of the sidewalk. Oh no, I got a better one for the dumbest thing you ever did: When you filled out a job application to go work with my friend, Donna, and you wrote really malicious stuff on the lie detector test. You got away with it then, but I think now the FBI would be after you [laughs].

Can you name 3 very important events in your life?
Sure. Uh…getting married, graduating college, oh, this is supposed to be up to 1995, right? OK, uh, graduating college, going to work for ABC News in New York and, um, losing a lot of weight.

What most explains why you are like you are?
Um, I think the combination of people I have known in my whole life.

What would I consider some of my favorite places?
Um, you?

Yes.
The art museum steps in Philly; um, any given rooftop on a dark city night; um, certain places on South Street, like, I think the Antiquarium, I think you're the one that turned me on to that place; uh, libraries, you've always really liked libraries; um…Spruce Street, Pine Street; uh…that's about all I can think of on those.

What are some of your favorite places?
Uh, some of the same: the art museum steps, South Street, some beaches in Florida, oh, wait back to 1994-95; um, Dominick's Tavern in Bellmawr, New Jersey; the Copa Banana on South Street; um, [exhalation] Penn's Landing at night; Parvin State Park in New Jersey; a couple places in Maine, the state of Maine; um, my grandmother's house…uh, one of the apartments that I lived in, the one at 20th and Spruce. Pretty much any part—there's a lot of parts of Center City: South Street, Chinatown, Philadelphia in general.

When was I probably most depressed?
After you broke up with Sue.

When was I probably most excited?
Um, [exhalation] I think you were very happy when you first most moved in with Trés, into that apartment, the Kribb…not having anything to do with Trés. That is when at, you know—you were just really fun and always seemed to be really, really up.

When were you most depressed?
Uh, in late—actually, um, a couple times—in 1994 I went through a period where I was pretty depressed. Um, and then the most depressed I had ever been was in 1999 when I lived in North Carolina. Oh, and even before that, sometimes on and off during high school.

When were you most excited?
Um, when I graduated college; when we all lived together in the house on 17th street; when I got the apartment at 20th and Spruce; um, when I first started working at Market Street Live!; um, when I was a sophomore in high school and I worked in the cowboy store, my first job—which was my first job, and it was my first job at the mall, in New Jersey [snicker]; um, setting up Spring Flings at Temple [University], um, and any other time I went to see a good band in Philly.

What would I consider my greatest achievements?
You, what would you consider your own greatest achievements? Um, traveling to Europe, by yourself; um, graduating college; um, getting over certain things that happened in your life; um, making the friends that you've made; living successfully on your own; uh, I think that's about it I can think of.

What would I consider my biggest regrets?
Hmm. I really don't know. Um, what would you regret, what did you regret? Uh, I can't imagine that you ever did anything to anybody that you regret, I can't imagine that you ever hurt anybody; [exhalation] maybe, I don't know, maybe that you didn't finish college sooner; um, maybe losing—probably knowing you—losing touch with some people you probably can't get in touch with again; um, maybe—I know you moved out of Center City—maybe you regretted that because you loved it so much. Uh, that's probably about it.

What are your greatest achievements?
Graduating college, going to work for ABC; um, at that time I could say that I maintained a very healthy social life and worked very hard. Um, my greatest achievements [exhalation] back to '94-95? Um, I don't know, uh, I was, uh—the time I was on *Remote Control* [MTV show]; um, doing some television anchoring for a cable station; um, greatest achievements: graduating school was pretty much the biggie for me. When I broke up with Andy I was very, very proud of that, very proud that I was, um, wise enough to not make that mistake. Um…I think that's about it.

What are your biggest regrets?
Giving away my cat, letting Andy have my cat, really, truly the only regret in life that I have.

What is some of my favorite music?
Uh, God. Mel Tormé, Led Zeppelin, um, classic rock in general, we both share the same kind of appreciation for that; um, let's see, anything on vinyl [laughs]; uh, I can't remember what it was, I can just say generally Rap because you were really into this rap song for awhile when we all lived together, and you kept saying "Bull dyking ass bitch" or whatever the thing was, the thing, and we corrected you on it. We

Theresa Collington

were saying, like, "Boon dagging ass bitch." Something that, like, Ice T or Ice Cube or whatever one of those militant rapper guys; um, let's see, what made Jim Tantum tag on that song? I just remember having a Led Zeppelin—like a Led Zeppelin sing-a-long at your house one night and singing Mel Tormé songs with you on the roof of your house. Um, stuff that's in—stuff that's in Woody Allen soundtracks, I think. [Exhalation.] That's about it. I never remember you as being much of an audiophile.

Can you name some of my dreams or goals?
Um, back in the '94 time probably not because we weren't talking very much: happiness probably, inner peace. Um, I really don't know what you were striving for back then, probably to finish this goddamn project, um, or any project that you were working on. Immediate goals, long term goals, I really don't know.

What are the most important things one can get out of living?
What are the most important things that one can get out of living?

Exactly.
That's going to make me cry. Happiness; fulfillment of their soul; um, to be loved for truly who you are by someone else; um, to be respected and appreciated at your place of employment; um, to find your soulmate; to have a job that—where they truly appreciate you and you appreciate them; to, um, have healthy relationships with people in your family; to have lots of good friends that, um—people that you enjoy their company, and they enjoy your company—basically friends that you love; um, and uh, although it's not a priority, but some degree of financial security. Um, I don't even remember what the question was now.

What are the most important things you can get out of living?
Oh yeah, um, a sense of—definitely, definitely—inner peace. To feel like you've done good and that you've made a mark on this world and that, um, you're loved; to be loved, actually.

Is working an evil necessity?
Fuck, yes!

Is it hard to be happy in life?
Yes, when you have to work, yes. It's not hard to be happy but it's hard to keep others from trying to make you unhappy.

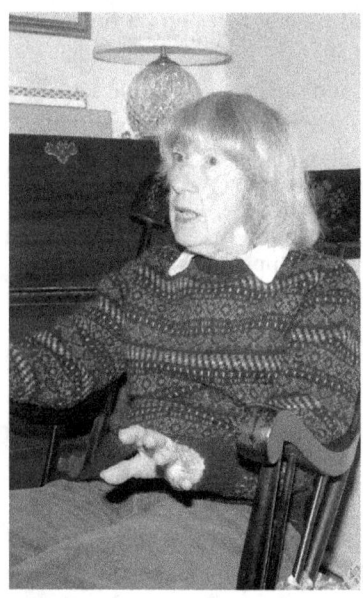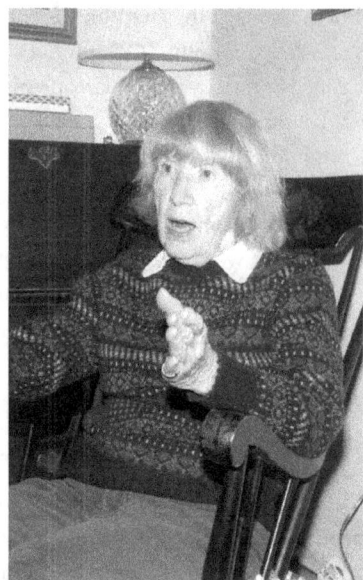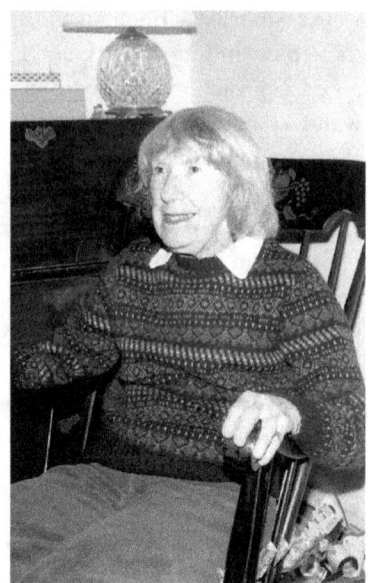

I interviewed Marie Davis, my grandmother, in her house.

How long have you known me?
From the day you were born, on.

How much do I weigh?
Now? I would say 140.

What color are my eyes?
Brownish-green.

How tall am I?
Five feet six.

Do you remember being a little kid?
Very well.

What is your earliest memory?
When I was two. Nobody believes that, but I can still see this stove in our kitchen. And on the hearth, which came out from the stove, was a box of Corn Flakes. I remember it well. And we didn't have a stove like that in any other house that we lived in.

Do you remember being 20 years old?

Around 20? Oh very well. I had finished college before I was twenty.

How was that possible?

I was 19 when I graduated.

So when did you start?

When I was 16.

Do you remember being 10 years old?

Very well.

Do you like getting older?

Not especially.

Who do I most look like, my mother or my father?

That's hard to say. I would say probably your father.

Of which do I share the most characteristics?

I don't know, I think you share characteristics of both.

What is your earliest memory of me?

Um, when you born. And then when you came back to, uh, New Jersey and when you were six weeks old and your mother had a gallbladder operation and she left at 2 am for the hospital. And you were left to me. You, a breast-fed baby. So I had to gather up, not only my wits, but some kind of thing to give you strength. So I gave you evaporated milk, diluted, and Karo added. Because I had read years ago that that's what the missionaries in foreign countries gave their children when they were babies.

Karo the syrup?

Karo the syrup, yes. And you lapped it up, no problem.

Can you name a few good qualities that I have?

Yes. You were a very easy child, adaptable, loved everybody. You were very easy to take care of. I had no problems with you.

But what about qualities now?

Oh, now. Well, I think you're a very thoughtful...interesting person to talk to and seem to be interested in other people and their opinions.

Can you name a few bad qualities or weaknesses that I have?

[Laughs.] Uh, I would say, and these are not bad qualities, but you seem diffident and rather unsure of yourself, as though you were willing to take second place to anyone else who wishes to pursue the space or the subject.

What in general are great qualities to have?
Well, I would say, first of all, an interest in other people...and, uh, a willingness to let someone else have center stage, and, uh, cheerfulness, and a willingness to help out, whatever the situation is.

Who do you admire or find inspirational?
I admire various people that I read about and, um, people who have written inspirational books, like Norman Vincent Peale and Howard Kushner and, uh, people like that. And I admired Eleanor Roosevelt when I read her life.

Are people at base good or bad?
Oh, good, definitely.

What are my hobbies?
Your hobbies? I really don't know enough to say but I suspect bike riding and painting, probably some of your books.

What are some of your favorite things?
Things not people. Piano, books, um, my car...cokes, cookies.

Who is the most famous person you've met?
Most famous that I've ever met. I can't think....some artist or musician that I went to a concert to hear I'm sure is probably the most famous one.

How many people are alive in the world?
Well, there are 240 million, supposedly, in the United States, and I don't know, but I would possibly say five billion.

Are you convinced of God's existence?
Definitely.

Do you think you have free will?
Yes, I do.

How do you deal with that?
Everyday I have a choice to make, to do this or not to, whatever it is.

How many ideas of how to live, or what life is about, are your own?
Well, I think when you are a child you are told what to do and how to live and as you grow older, teenage,

college age. And then when I was married I remember thinking I could do as I please. And I think, uh, as you become an adult, you make all your own decisions within the bounds of the law of the land.

Do you remember a time when I wasn't around?
Yes.

Can you name 3 very important events in my life?
In your life? Well, I don't know how important you would consider them, but I would imagine, um, your move from Florida to New Jersey was one of them. And perhaps—when you came up here you lived first with us, then with your folks in Bordentown and then you had an apartment in Penn Park—and perhaps the next most important thing was your move to Willingboro where you had a house and a room of your own. And perhaps the day you entered school was an important day in your life.

College or first grade?
No, first grade.

What most explains why I am like I am?
You are the way you are because of your parents and the way you were brought up and your environment, what you were exposed to...your schools and your friends.

Do I look different from when you first met me?
Of course, [laughs] very different.

What is the dumbest thing I've done?
The dumbest thing you've ever done? Oh, I don't know...I have no idea except that one time, when you were here, you tried to get in the door by ramming the door with a stick, a metal door. [Laughs.] That's the only thing that I can remember.

Can you name 3 very important events in your life?
I would say graduation from college, and getting married and...maybe getting our first house, that's Concord Circle.

When was I probably most depressed?
I don't know but I suspect in your college days when you had to repeat something.

When was I probably most excited?
Perhaps on your graduation; I don't know that either.

What would I consider my greatest achievements?
I would imagine getting out on your own, getting an apartment, and getting a job. Becoming independent, in other words.

What would I consider my biggest regrets?
I haven't talked to you about your regrets. Possibly a regret that you didn't get the first job you applied for.

Can you name some of my favorite music?
Nope, don't think I could.

Can you name some of my dreams or goals?
Well, I haven't heard you discuss them but I should imagine having a better job would be a goal. And, uh, a dream of being successful in whatever it is you're undertaking.

What are the most important things one can get out of living?
Happiness, friendship, new experiences.

Is working an evil necessity?
It's a necessity but it certainly isn't evil.

Is it hard to be happy in life?
No.

Do you remember me as a baby?
Yes.

Do you remember anything else from what you said?
Oh yes, many other things. Uh, you were a cute little kid and loved cats, I remember that. And I couldn't keep you all the time when you were first with me because I had to go to work. So I took you in a basket to my friend Joanne Bertozzi and she kept you while I was at work. Then I picked you up as soon as I came home from work because your mother was ill, she had to stay in the hospital, you know.

Gallbladder?
Gallbladder, yes.

From what I used to look like, does it follow that I should look like this, what I look like now?
I dare say.

What most explains why you are like you are?
I think my heritage, that is, who my parents and grandparents were and the environment in which I lived, explains why I am this way. So it is heredity and environment.

What would I consider some of my favorite places?
Your favorite places? I would think our backyard where you played and spent the night out in the yard one

night; and I would think your porch in one of the houses where you lived when you had one half and Julie had the other half. That was your playroom.

What are some of your favorite places?
My favorite place right now is the back porch that is lovely and sunny and breezy and comfortable. And another favorite place is the seashore. And the most beautiful place I ever went to was Muir Woods [California]. That is where the great, tall Redwoods are.

When were you most depressed?
I was most depressed at the death of my mother, at the death of my third daughter, and at the death of my husband and at the death of my fourth daughter. *Death* is the most depressing thing I have ever experienced.

When were you most excited?
When I graduated from college and when I got married and when we got our first house.

Who are some of my close friends?
Your close friends?...I guess your next door neighbor, the child who lived next door was probably—and then when you got older, I'm not sure, because I was not living with you then.

What are some of my favorite things?
I guess your pets, cats. Or your bike.

What are your greatest achievements?
First, having four daughters, uh, making lots of good friends, and getting a house the way I wanted it.

What does that mean?
That means having it in the style I like both inside and out: furnishing it, landscaping it.

Anything else?
[Pause.] It is hard to say you have achieved anything if you have no notable result of your effort. Having nine grandchildren is a great thing but I did not achieve that....I guess getting our house paid for was a considerable achievement.

What are your biggest regrets?
[Pause.] I hardly know. I try not to think about regrets. I regret a little that we didn't insist upon all four children finishing college. And...I regret I didn't encourage Frank more to go on with his college work. But we were so strapped for money and it was hard for him when he was working all day to take these grad-uate courses in New York.

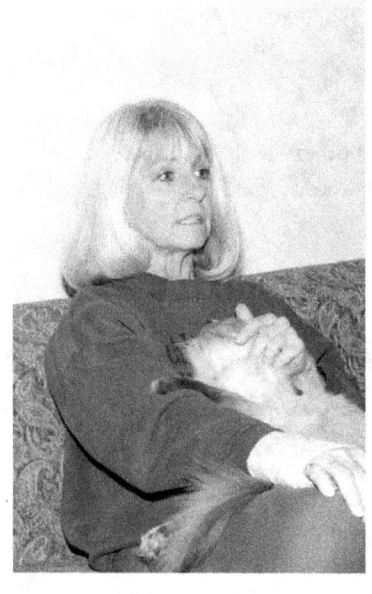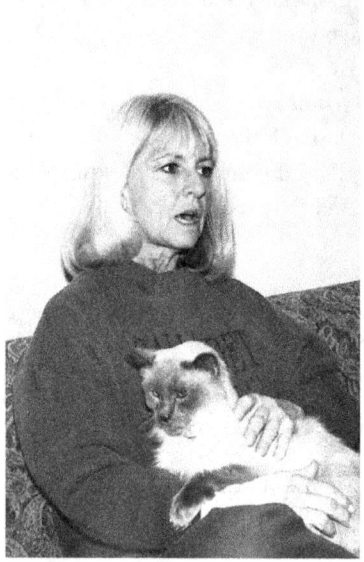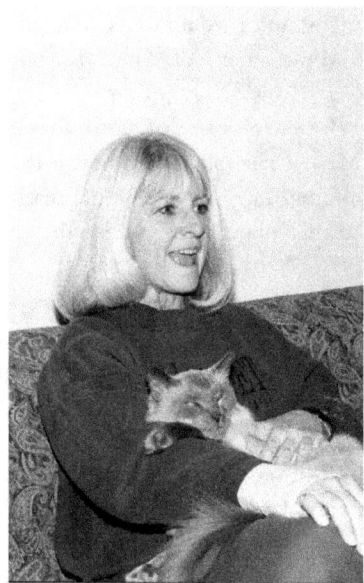

I interviewed Penni Davis-Tantum, my mother, in her house.

How long have you known me?
All your life.

How much do I weigh?
About 130.

What color are my eyes?
Brown.

How tall am I?
Five-six, five-six and a half.

Do you remember being a little kid?
Some.

What is your earliest memory?
I don't know.

What's an early memory?
One of my earliest memories—although I have glimpses and I have no idea of the age—was Mimi [her mother] pushing us up the street in this big, humongous stroller, a wicker stroller. Um, I don't know how old I was.

Were you in it?
Yes.

So it was more than one of you?
Well, it was probably Adrienne and me. I don't know whether the stroller was for one or two could fit in it. I don't even know that.

Do you remember being 20 years old?
Twenty, uh, you were, ooh, nineteen and a half...you were between six months and a year old when I was twenty. So I remember more in relation to you than to me.

Do you remember being 10 years old?
Not really.

Do you remember being in fifth grade?
No, I don't remember fifth grade. I remember third grade because I liked my teacher. I remember kindergarten because I used to draw pictures for other than just our class.

Do you like getting older?
[Laughs.] Oh, but of course I just love getting old. No. Well, to a point. I mean I think forty would be the ideal age to stay at.

Did you always used to think that?
Of course not.

What did you used to think the ideal age would be?
Probably thirty. Well, probably, I never really thought about it much.

Did you think about earlier than that ?
Well, when I was younger I'm sure I thought whatever age it was was ideal.

Really, even when you were ten?
No, no, no, no, no. When you're little you want to be a grown-up.

Who do I most look like, you or my father?
Our side of the family, not your father's.

Of which do I share the most characteristics?
Well, you have some of both of us. For instance, your lack of sense of direction is your father, through and through. Some of your mannerisms, I guess, are your father. Your bad eyesight and your crooked teeth are your father [laughs].

So are you going to say that it's mainly that side with the most similar characteristics?
Uh, I'm not sure. Your lack of showing emotion—I don't know what side of the family that is from. I don't know. I would say it would have to be split.

What is your earliest memory of me?
Being pregnant with you.

Can you name a few good qualities that I have?
Oh, you're a terrific person. You have lots of good qualities.

Anything specific?
Um...I hope you're honest, you seem to be, forthright. Those are extremely important, I think. Um, you're bright. You're nice-looking, I mean, I don't know what else you want. Those are important things I think.

Can you name a few bad qualities or weaknesses that I have?
Yes, you don't show emotion, that's not good. It's not good to keep it inside. You're stubborn, of course you get that honestly but...and in some things you are set in your ways even though you're too young to be set in your ways; when you've made up your mind about something it's like a steel trap.

What in general are five great qualities to have?
Honesty, sincerity, intelligence...being, um, I don't know that I want to the full extent of extroverted, but being able to speak and get along with people even if you don't know them. Um, honesty, integrity, did I say integrity? Alright, well, that should be five.

Who do you admire or find inspirational?
I don't know.

Are people at base good or bad?
I think there is some good in everybody.

So, largely good?
I would say yes.

What are my hobbies?
Your hobbies? Projects. Off the wall projects, like the oatmeal book, your *Hairpiece*, your—whatever your medicine cabinet thing is. Art, I would say is a hobby for you. And now, well, no, you really haven't started dabbling in the car yet much enough to call it a hobby. I don't know what else.

Who are some of my close friends?
I would say Aram, Jack, Jackie, uh, Doug, I don't know; David of course. And I don't know who else. Maybe Roger, but I don't know how close he is anymore.

What are some of my favorite things?
Books. Um...I don't know.

What are some of your favorite things?
Mine? My cats, the dog, you and Julie, needless to say.

Who is the most famous person you've met?
I don't know.

How many people are alive in the world?
I don't know.

No guess?
What, 300 million? I have no idea.

Are you convinced of God's existence?
Absolutely.

Do you think you have free will?
Yes.

How do you deal with that?
Life is choices. And you make your choices. Everything is a choice. Not making a choice is a choice.

How many ideas of how to live, or what life is about, are your own?
Probably none, because I'm sure everybody had them before me. But they are mine if I have to choose to have those and follow those.

Do you remember a time when I wasn't around?
Yes.

Can you name 3 very important events in my life?
Important events? Your birth, your high school graduation, your college graduation....They're all important events.

What most explains why I am like I am?
Well, I don't know what most explains it. Some of it comes from who your parents are. Some of it comes from how you were brought up. Some of it, I think, is innate.

Do I look different from when you first met me?
Yes, you do. You were seven pounds two ounces when I first met you and had lots of dark, dark—almost

black—hair.

What is the dumbest thing I've done?
Oh, well, I don't know that I can name anything right off the top of my head. Ah! I can name one thing, when you were driving the Maverick and the wheel fell off [laughs]. That was a dumb thing.

What would I consider some of my favorite places?
Some of your favorite places? Museums, um...libraries. I don't know, I don't know.

When was I probably most depressed?
I don't know because you don't show.

When was I probably most excited?
Good question.

What would I consider my greatest achievements?
College graduation, going to Europe. I don't know.

What would I consider my biggest regrets?
Well, either not getting a job that you wanted to do, or not going on to grad school yet.

What is some of my favorite music?
Your favorite music? I don't know what you like in music. Maybe some New Age, but I don't know. Some—oh, classical. I know you like classical.

Can you name some of my dreams or goals?
No. Well, to get the MG up and running, that would be one. I hope one would be to get a good job that you like.

What are the most important things one can get out of living?
Knowledge, experience, um...a broader view of life and people, new interests. Just a broader perspective of everything.

Do you remember what I was like before puberty?
Yeah, you were a good—you were always a good kid. Um...you were, well, you had friends but you weren't wild or anything. You were pretty good. You were pretty obedient and trustworthy.

Do you remember what it felt like when I was in the womb?
Oh, I felt you kicking and that sort of thing. I liked very much being pregnant.

Penni Davis-Tantum

Did you carry me for nine months?
Yes, I did.

Do you remember me as a little kid?
Yes. You were wonderful, you were great. You were bright, you'd go off and you'd wander around and visit people and...you were curious.

Does he exist anymore?
The little kid? Uh, I think there's a little bit of little kid in everybody. I don't think—we'll...I don't know. I don't think we all ever fully grow up.

What did he lose as he aged?
Probably spontaneity, um...somewhat, somewhat. People tend to become more conservative when they get older, they become—they tend to become more inhibited...because they're afraid they are going to look foolish or that sort of thing.

What are some of your favorite places?
Colorado, Grand Caymen, um...San Francisco.

When were you most depressed?
Ever since July of this year.

When were you most excited?
Probably from February to July this year.

Can you name 3 very important events in your life?
Important in what way?

Important in affecting your life.
I guess my marriage was one of them, it affected my life. Um...my sisters' and father's deaths affected me... and grandpa's death, when I was in Texas.

What most explains why you are like you are?
[Laughs.] I haven't a clue.

What are your greatest achievements?
My two kids.

What are your biggest regrets?
Not having remarried, um...I don't know.

Is working an evil necessity?

Working? Yes and no.

Why so?

Yes, because I never wanted that, I didn't have—I was not ambitious, I didn't have ambitious goals. No, it's not because you have to work to survive, to get the things you want. And people *have* to have a roof over their head, and they *have* to have food and something to wear. It's not all just materialistic—having to have stuff. It's a necessity.

Is it hard to be happy in life?

Probably not. I don't—it depends on your outlook....No, it's not hard.

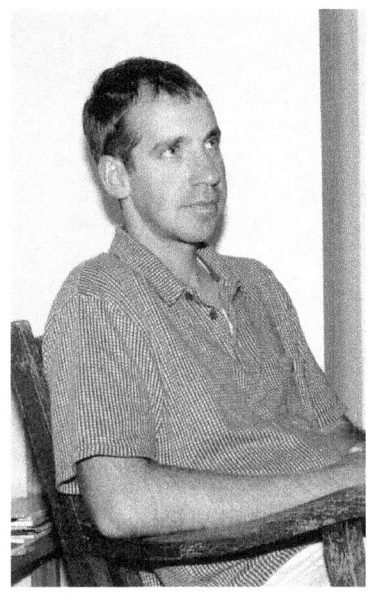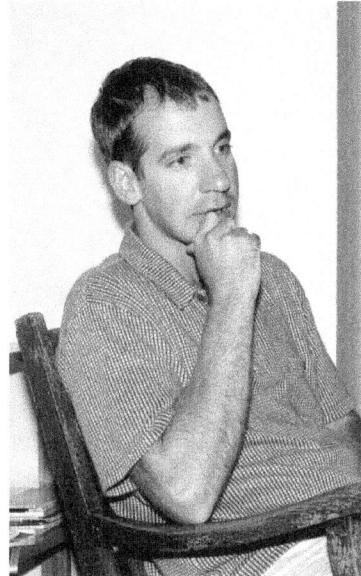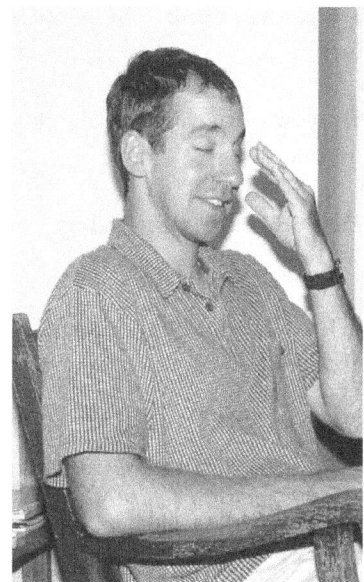

I interviewed John C. Frederick, my friend, in my apartment and later on my front steps.

How long have you known me?
I've known you since 1988, seven years.

How much do I weigh?
I'd say you weigh about...145 pounds.

What color are my eyes?
Hazel, brown.

How tall am I?
Five-four.

How well do you know me?
All too well.

Do you remember being a little kid?
Yes, I do.

What is your earliest memory?
My earliest memory was when I was in the baby carriage going across the train tracks in Lansdale. I think I was two or three.

Do you remember being 20 years old?
Yes.

Do you remember being 10 years old?
More or less.

Do you like getting older?
In some ways I do.

Who do I most look like, my mother or my father?
Well, you don't look like your mother and I've never seen your father, so I would assume you look like your father.

Of which do I share the most characteristics?
I don't know but I would say I have a feeling that...you're probably more like your dad.

What is your earliest memory of me?
Earliest memory of you is...hanging out with you and Trés at the Kribb [Trés and my apartment]. But I can't remember a specific day. But just being there at the Kribb, probably sometime in 1988.

Can you name a few good qualities that I have?
A few, several? As many as I can? Um, you're a good listener, you're objective, you're intelligent and you're reasonable.

Can you name a few bad qualities or weaknesses that I have?
You seem to be stuck in a rut—no productivity just like the rest of us [laughs]. Um...that's about it.

What in general are great qualities to have?
For anyone? Great qualities are...somebody who can be understanding, somebody who can be a good listener, somebody who can be supportive...intelligent, although that is more or less built in I think. Good qualities or great qualities: it's somebody who is aware of other people's needs, or other people's concerns, or...other people's way of seeing and thinking.

Who do you admire or find inspirational?
That's living or not living? Anybody? Probably Corbu [Le Corbusier]...any of the pioneers of...Modernism. Specifically, people like Jackson Pollack, Jasper Johns. More or less abstract modernists, painting... Andy Warhol. I guess you could say the artist...the artist that could see the world in a new fashion. Especially the modernists, people that pioneered Modernism.

Are people at base good or bad?
I would say good.

What are my hobbies?

Your hobbies are doing projects, going to New York, looking at women...and reading.

Who are some of my close friends?

Me [laughs], Don Mumford, Doug, Shilpa, Sherone, Aram....Those are—I think those are your closest friends.

What are some of my favorite things?

Things as in material or things to do?

It's open to your interpretation.

Your favorite things are probably...items of pop culture: Silly Putty...strange goggles, display racks, display items, '60s cars, '70s cars...things with a lot of character. Things with—let's say '60s and '70s culture with a lot of character.

What are some of your favorite things?

Certainly, design objects, things that are made with care...exotic cars, things that are well-designed...things that look good but also have an important function.

Who is the most famous person you've met?

Probably Mike Schmidt.

How many people are alive in the world?

Four billion.

Are you convinced of God's existence?

I would say for the most part. I think everybody has doubts. I think if we didn't have doubts we wouldn't be here. And we need to be here to be totally convinced.

Do you think you have free will?

I have free will but only within my own limitations, my own personal limitations...and...governmental limitations.

Can you explain your "own personal limitations."

Yeah, my fears. I can go as far as my fears allow me to.

How do you deal with your free will?

How do I deal with it? How do I use it?

How is it that you can acknowledge you have it and reconcile that?

Because sometimes I can go beyond my own fear and decide—and find out that...what I can do is actually beyond my initial conceived limitations; because I think the only boundaries that you have are the ones you put on yourself.

How many ideas of how to live, or what life is about, are your own?
Well, it's hard to say what is my own. I don't know if other people thought of it before or not. I would assume they did. I think most ideas are just regurgitated. I think most ideas about life are just floating around in the air, just like any other creative idea. They're waiting to be picked out.

Do you remember a time when I wasn't around?
Yes.

Can you name 3 important events in my life?
When you graduated from Temple, when you got a meaningful job at World Game, or worked at a meaningful place...and when you decided that your MGA would be salvageable [laughs], a realistic goal. Going to Europe.

What most explains why I am like I am?
I don't think I've known you long enough to know that. It's probably a combination of your parents and your own innate personality.

Do I look different from when you first met me?
No, I think you look pretty much the same.

What is the dumbest thing I've done?
You were working in a restaurant and you wanted to tell somebody [laughs] to go get a plate for the salad bar, because you were working in a Saladalley, and you forgot the word for "plate."

Can you name 3 important events in your life?
Graduation from college, going to Europe, learning French and getting my designs to together.

What are your biggest regrets?
I would say not dealing with my...health sooner.

What is some of my favorite music?
B-52s, the album with "Rock Lobster"...Brasil '66, Beatles.

Can you name some of my dreams or goals?
Have enough money to go to Europe once a year, finish the MGA...to have a girlfriend, and to have a nicer apartment with hot water and lots of pressure—uh, hot water pressure that is.

John C. Frederick

What are the most important things one can get out of living?
Understanding why we are here, or getting closer to a better understanding of that; understanding other people's perspective and understanding the concept of family.

Is working an evil necessity?
It's a necessity but a good necessity. People need to feel productive...and they also forget about problems they may have after working for eight or ten hours, or six hours. It makes them feel accomplished, or it should—if they are doing something they feel good about.

Is it hard to be happy in life?
If you start out being happy...and you are in the habit of being happy, no, it's not hard. But if you're unhappy, in the habit of being unhappy, or used to being unhappy, it's difficult to get into that habit. But once you...get yourself in that routine—if that's possible—then it's not too difficult.

Is it hard for you to be happy in life?
It used to be but not so much anymore...because I'm in the habit of being happy.

What most explains why you are like you are?
I think it's a combination of my environment—50% my environment and 50% genetics and what I got from my parents.

What would I consider some of my favorite places?
The woods. Um...your apartment...and, three?...That's all I can think of.

When was I probably most depressed?
Probably most depressed after breaking up with Sue; afterwards you felt a little discouraged about the girl-friend thing and your job situation wasn't that great.

What are some of your favorite places?
The woods and your apartment [laughs]. I certainly like the woods, my shop....I like the Wharton Esherick Museum, which is out near Valley Forge Park. And I like Amsterdam.

When was I probably most excited?
You were most excited right before you went on your Europe trip.

When were you most depressed?
I would say during high school, during the entire high school [laughs]. But also after Rachel left and we broke up.

When were you most excited?
I was most excited when I was traveling around Europe.

What would I consider my greatest achievements?

Traveling to Europe...graduating from college...and the *Hairpiece* frame [laughs].

What would I consider my biggest regrets?

I don't know.

What are your greatest achievements?

Learning French, getting my shop together, graduating from school, traveling to Europe.

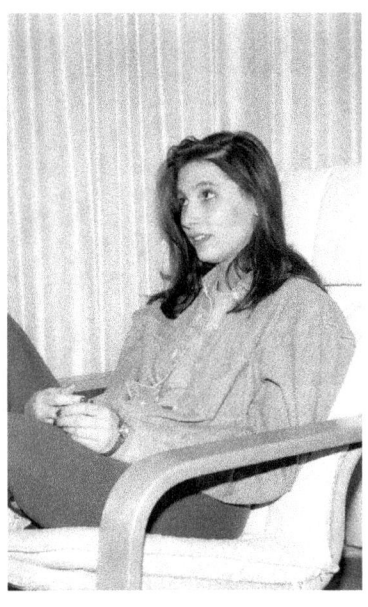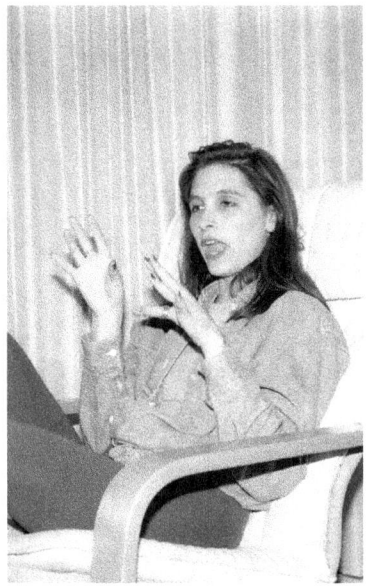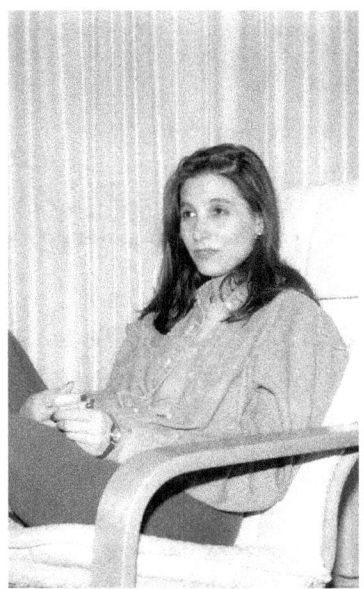

I interviewed Jacqueline Glassman, my friend, in her apartment.

How long have you known me?
Eleven years.

How much do I weigh?
I would say 142.

What color are my eyes?
Hmm, greenish.

How tall am I?
Not taller than I am [laughs]. You are 5 foot, uh, 4 inches.

How well do you know me?
Very.

Do you remember being a little kid?
A little bit.

What is your earliest memory?
I think of moving from Philadelphia to Yardley, so I was like three years old.

Do you remember being 20 years old?
Yeah.

Do you remember being 10 years old?
Not specifically, but I'm sure there are some things I remember.

Do you like getting older?
Not particularly.

Who do I most look like, my mother or my father?
Um, well, I haven't seen your father as much as your mother, so I'll say your mother.

Of which do I share the most characteristics?
Probably your father.

What is your earliest memory of me?
[Laughs.] Um, probably at, well—I don't remember what came first—but at Doug's graduation party probably. But I think there may have been one other night when we did something. But no, I'll say that.

Can you name a few good qualities that I have?
[Laughs.] Deadly silence. "Wait a minute, this isn't how it's supposed to go." Um, funny, um, good friend, loyal...how many am I supposed to give? Oh that's right, you can't talk. Uh, I'll stop there.

Can you name a few bad qualities or weaknesses that I have?
Um...let's see, um, kind of a procrastinator, but not really a procrastinator, just kind of, like, not finishing stuff, maybe. Um, what else?...not interested in money enough. [Laughs.] That's enough bad qualities.

Are you done?
Yeah.

What in general are great qualities to have?
Um, funny; um, quick, although that probably goes with funny; um...loyal; smart.

Who do you admire or find inspirational?
Nobody.

Are people at base good or bad?
Good.

What are my hobbies?
Crazy projects like this one [laughs]. Um, what are your hobbies? Bike riding, when your knee isn't bad,

um, on and off working out, um, different projects like I said, um...some interest in music.

Who are some of my close friends?
Hmm, Aram, Jack, Sherone, me, I hope, Doug, um, who else? Um...I'd say those are the closest.

What are some of my favorite things?
Favorite things? You can't be more specific than that?

No, it's really what makes sense to you.
Um, favorite things, um...hmm, well, I guess probably riding your bike; um, skiing, when you can get to do it; um, certain art stuff; being a little weird; um...that's it.

What are some of your favorite things?
Shopping [laughs]; um, being outside; just hanging out with my friends; um, that's it.

Who is the most famous person you've met?
That I've met. Who have I met? I might have to think about this for a minute. [Pause.] Lorne Michaels.

How many people are alive in the world?
[Exhalation.] Three and a half billion.

Are you convinced of God's existence?
Convinced? No.

But?
But it's very possible, I'm just not 100% sure. But there is a very good chance.

Do you think you have free will?
Yes.

How do you deal with that?
I think you have to take responsibility for your own actions, and not—you can't blame everything on other people, which some people tend to do some of the time.

How many ideas of how to live, or what life is about, are your own?
Completely my own? Probably very few because I don't think I have some independent philosophy like some people might have. So I'd have to say none, because I don't think I have got some totally different philosophy that nobody's ever thought of before.

Do you remember a time when I wasn't around?
[Laughs.] Yes, sorry [laughs]. My earliest memory begins with meeting Jim [laughs]. Then God created

Jim.

Can you name 3 very important events in my life?
Three very important events. Ah, graduating from college, your parents divorcing, and starting your job at World Game.

What most explains why I am like I am?
[Laughs.] Sure, you don't want to go into analysis so you try to interview people. Um, what most explains it? I would say it has to do with your parents getting divorced, probably, and, probably, your mom having to take care of you guys and your dad not being around, and whatever your life was like then, probably. Although some of it has to be your basic personality too because stuff like that can't affect you completely.

Do I look different from when you first met me?
Not a lot, I mean your hair's longer.

What is the dumbest thing I've done?
[Laughs.] How much is left on this? What is the dumbest thing you've done? Um, not going to your math final in college. I think that's pretty dumb.

Can you name 3 very important events in your life?
In my life? Three important events, hmm...um, three important events. Um...meeting Andy, probably; um...an event, maybe my Bas Mitzvah, although it's not very important to me now; um, and probably starting working.

What most explains why you are like you are?
I thought I was going to avoid this one; I was hoping we might skip over this. Um, probably a lot of is, you know, the way my parents were when I was growing up, um, some of it is the way other people treated me. But I think a lot of it is just kind of your basic personality, cause I—I mean I can remember sort of thinking the same stuff a long time ago that I think now and, you know, you know being funny when I was little or, you know, stuff like that.

What would I consider some of my favorite places?
Favorite places, hmm? You want to stop it so I can think about it? [Pause.] Um, Jim's favorite places...not a lot I can think of. I don't think you have ever gone on a vacation somewhere and come back and said it was, like, totally awesome, it was like, "It was OK." Um, Philadelphia Library, certain museums sometimes, probably the beach generically, no specific beach, although you don't really go anymore. Um, that's all I can think of. I can't really think—you don't really say, like, "I really love this place."

What are some of your favorite places?
Um, almost any beach that's really warm and nice, um...there's a lot of places: Los Angeles; um, Palm Springs; um, where we went skiing in Colorado last year, at Beaver Creek, which is where we stayed; um,

Las Vegas...that's it.

When was I probably most depressed?

Most depressed? Hmm, um, do I have to pick one?

No.

Um...yeah, now I'll like totally bum you out by reciting every depressing thing ever [laughs], "I can't go on with this interview." Maybe when, like, 18 people in your family died and then you got fired from Capriccio [laughs] like all in a month. Nice of me to bring that one up. Um, what else?....It could be over a woman, although I'm not sure which woman you'd be the most depressed over. I don't care to say anymore.

When was I probably most excited?

Most excited, hmm. [Exhalation.] You never get excited [laughs]. Um, when were you most excited? Um...maybe when you were going to go to Europe, um, I'd say that.

When were you most depressed?

Probably when a boy did something bad to me.

When were you most excited?

Hmm, think you never get excited [laughs]. When was I most excited? Um, when was I happy, most excited? I never get excited, that's my problem. Um...I don't know, I don't know.

What would I consider my greatest achievements?

Um, probably the projects that you finished; um...yeah, all the projects that you finished. Doing your sister's wedding pictures maybe; um...maybe some of the stuff you're doing at work now, because you are doing stuff that's different than stuff that you've ever done before; um, graduating college, finally. That's it.

What would I consider my biggest regrets?

Hmm...biggest regrets? Um, maybe not having as good relationships with members of your family as you could have, being maybe more distant from them than you should be; um, letting opportunities pass by because you...just are kind of thinking about it and you think you're going to do it, you think you're going to do it, and then it's, like, too late; um, maybe...not being...as outgoing a friend as you could be with some of your friends, although I wouldn't say that is the case anymore. Just kind of waiting for people to come to you maybe, but I wouldn't say that anymore; and uh, not getting Laura Garrett [laughs]. I know you too well [laughs]. "Ix-nay on the aura-lay arrett-gay."

What are your greatest achievements?

Hmm, my greatest achievements? Um, my greatest achievements? Being a good daughter; um, doing well in school; doing well in work; being a good friend to some people; um, that's it.

What are your biggest regrets?
My biggest regrets? Um, probably going to Penn [University of Pennsylvania]; um, not being as good a friend as I could be to some people; sort of abandoning friendships sometimes, not pursuing them as much as I should; um, being mean to people in my family; being mean to my boyfriend; not being a very good person sometimes.

What is some of my favorite music?
I really have no idea anymore; I really don't know.

Can you name some of my dreams or goals?
Dreams or goals? Um, hmm...well, you probably have other projects that you eventually want to do or finish; um, maybe to make more stuff with wood or whatever you made those things before, finish those or sell those. Um, dreams or goals? Um...have a new girlfriend.

What are the most important things one can get out of living?
Um, happiness, love, companionship, friendship and family.

Is working an evil necessity?
Definitely. Although hopefully not forever [laughs].

Is it hard to be happy in life?
I think it's different for different people. Some people are very easily pleased and are just basically happy, other people are basically less happy. So It depends on what your basic personality is.

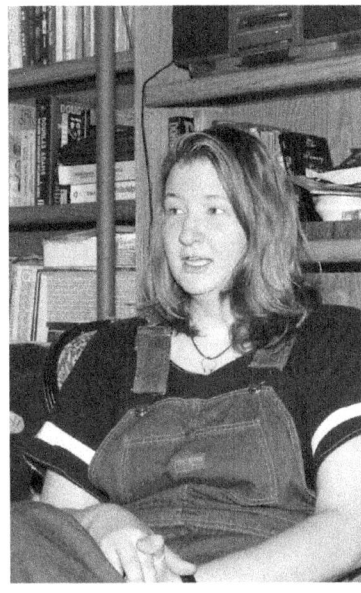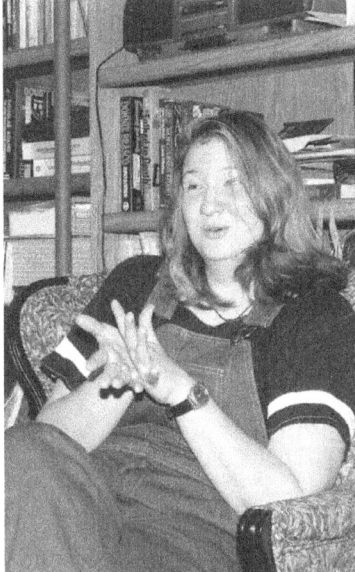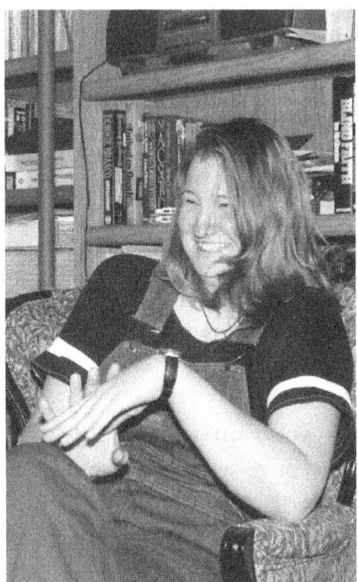

I interviewed Sue Lerch, my friend and ex-girlfriend, in her house.

How long have you known me?
Um...since 1989, actually. Do you want me to elaborate? [Laughs.]

How much do I weigh?
Uh, do you want me to guess right now?

Yes.
Well, 'cause I haven't seen you, like, in a while. Alright. Stand up and twirl [laughs]. Um, I don't know, you look pretty fit, 140?

What color are my eyes?
Oh, no. Uh, hazel, brown? Brown or hazel.

How tall am I?
[Laughs.] Five-four and a half.

How well do you know me?
How well? I think pretty well.

Do you remember being a little kid?
Not the entirety of it. I remember parts of it.

What is your earliest memory?

[Pause.] You know, I think my earliest memory is, um, the earliest event that I remember...is when we used to shop at Pantry Pride with my mom and a sign fell on my head [laughs], because I thought that because I stared at the sign it fell on my head. And I remember my sister and I used to, like, we thought that the Pantry Pride check out guy was really cute and he rescued me.

How old were you?

[Laughs.] I don't even know, like, seven maybe. No, I don't remember, young.

Do you remember being 20 years old?

Yeah.

Do you remember being 10 years old?

Are you trying to regress me? [Laughs.] Ten, hold on...yeah, I guess, yeah, vaguely.

Do you like getting older?

You know, theoretically I like getting older [laughs], but whenever my birthday rolls around I get depressed, it's just weird.

Who do I most look like, my mother or my father?

Uh, I think you most look like your mother, but I have seen your mother more.

Of which do I share the most characteristics?

Your father.

What is your earliest memory of me?

Of you? Well probably when we worked at Capriccio, the coffee shop, and, um, and you wore your Silly Putty glasses [laughs] of course.

Can you name a few good qualities that I have?

Um, well, yes I can, but I have to think. A few good qualities: oh, well, kind to animals [laughs]. Um, I don't know, you're very creative and smart and...and nice, I mean not really nice, not nice like some people, but—and thoughtful, which I think is important.

Can you name a few bad qualities or weaknesses that I have?

Oh sure. Let's see, weaknesses; I think that you're insecure of your abilities, I think that you don't give yourself enough credit? Not really credit, but I think follow through...on projects and things. And also something that's not really a fault, but that I found very annoying, was the documenting everything. Not annoying, just weird.

Sue Lerch

What in general are great qualities to have?
[Exhalation.] I think...great qualities to have, well, it's always good to be nice to people no matter what, 'cause I think that's very hard. And I also think doing what you say is a great quality and, uh, that's probably it [laughs].

Who do you admire or find inspirational?
I don't know. Uh...nobody, I don't know.

Are people at base good or bad?
Didn't we have this discussion before? Uh, at base? Well, I think they're both. I don't know.

What are my hobbies?
Your hobbies? [Laughs.] Um, masturbation, [laughs] I don't know. Your hobbies, well your old hobbies used to be...documentation of things, uh...I don't know, bike riding...projects, I guess, if they're hobbies.

Who are some of my close friends?
Aram, Sherone, um, at the time—you know, I can't remember this guy's name, the Tyler school guy, oh, you can't answer; uh, I guess that's it; your mom.

What are some of my favorite things?
Just your favorite things in general? Some of your favorite things. I don't know. Uh, that big white sweater you used to have, you loved that. Oh, and your gray sweatpants, you used to love them. Your gray sweatpants, you wore them like every day [laughs] and your bike is always one of your favorite things. Eh, that's it I guess.

What are some of your favorite things?
My favorite things? Well, you know I've tried to examine the constant things that I've always had favorites of, like, since I was little, because they're constantly changing, and the only two things that I have liked since I was little is ice cream and orange juice. And that's it. So that's going to be my answer.

Who is the most famous person you've met?
Uh...[exhalation] it was, you know what, it was at Capriccio, it was this boxer guy and I forget his name [laughs].

How many people are alive in the world?
How many? Five billion. Do you mean alive as in breathing or as alive really? I don't know. Five billion, isn't that the world thing?

Are you convinced of God's existence?
Am I convinced of it? Yes.

Do you think you have free will?

You know, I have been thinking about this a lot, as usual. Do I think I have free will? To a point I do. Um...nyah, I mean, sort of.

How do you deal with that?

How do I deal with that? Well, I try to be aware of it. I try to—I try to be aware that I probably have no free will and, I don't know; I don't deal with it very well.

How many ideas of how to live, or what life is about, are your own?

How many ideas ever?

Yes.

OK. Uh, well, you know what is weird is whenever I think that I've invented something it turns out that somebody already thought of it still. Actually, I just had one recently, so one and I think it's my own.

Do you remember a time when I wasn't around?

Yeah! [Laughs.]

Can you name 3 very important events in my life?

Three very important events. Your birth, you mean events that you remember. OK. Probably the death of [aunt] Jeanne; um, going away to Europe; and...I don't know, maybe leaving Capriccio. I'm just talking about the span that I knew you, I don't know really before. Oh, wait can I change that? Your parents' divorce.

What most explains why I am like I am?

[Exhalation.] Well, you know I've actually given this much thought and I think that psychologically analyzing you, I think that because your parents' divorced and you were so young, I think there was this weird, like, "I'm responsible, I'm not responsible" thing. I mean I think eighty—I think, like, maybe 85 to 90% of you is just the way that you are, the way that you were born, like a freak. But then I think the other 10 to 15% is a product of your parents' divorce, because I think it's a definite weirdness, like, with your mom and, like, you were, like, the man of the house because you had a sister, but then you were kind of just too young. You know what I mean? Well, you don't have to.

Do I look different from when you first met me?

Actually, I don't think you do, minus the Silly Putty glasses, of course.

What is the dumbest thing I've done?

The dumbest thing you've done. I don't even know, I have no idea; I can't think of anything really, like, dumb that you've done.

Can you name 3 very important events in your life?
In my life? Well, [exhalation]...I suppose it would be moving out of my house, dropping out of school, and having Sophie, well, and starting to paint also.

What most explains why you are like you are?
Hmm...you know I attribute most of mine to my upbringing. Because everything that I am now I can look back and see that I was either taught it or that it was some, like, malformation of what my parents were trying to teach me.

What would I consider some of my favorite places?
Your favorite places? Uh, the park. Mostly anything outdoors, I think.

What are some of your favorite places?
My favorite places? Um, my house, I don't know, any ice cream store.

When was I probably most depressed?
You know I actually think...I don't think—as far as I could see you didn't go through, like—well, no. I think during maybe the whole three years of our relationship you were kind of depressed. But I think mostly after you came back from Europe, kind of. And I can understand why, because God, it's depressing to come back to the United States. That's it I guess.

When was I probably most excited?
Excited? Well, I don't know, you had, like, bouts of being excited when you would think of a new project.

When were you most depressed?
When was I most depressed? In my whole life? Um, right after I moved out of my house, my parents' house.

When were you most excited?
I don't know. Probably now am I most excited.

What would I consider my greatest achievements?
You? Uh, you know what, I don't know what you would, but I think it would be the *Hairpiece* project and the, uh, art museum thing. The art museum—where you went into the art museum and hung the picture on the wall.

What would I consider my biggest regrets?
Biggest regrets? Uh, I don't know. I guess...not going to more school, maybe. I don't know.

More school?
Uh, no not like Moore College of Art, like more, m-o-r-e. You know, going on for a graduate degree.

What are your greatest achievements?
I don't know, I don't think I've done them yet.

What are your biggest regrets?
My biggest regrets? You know I don't really have any.

What is some of my favorite music?
James Taylor [laughs]. Uh, you know I don't know anymore now. Anything that Woody Allen thinks [laughs].

Can you name some of my dreams or goals?
Your dreams or goals? Well, you know...I don't know if we really even discussed that. I mean I knew that you were doing projects and things like that to get to an end or to...[exhalation] figure something out, I guess. But I don't know what your real goal is.

What are the most important things one can get out of living?
[Exhalation.] I think just the experience of it, I think just the pleasure. I think the most important thing about living is to not affect somebody else's life in a negative way.

Is working an evil necessity?
[Exhalation.] I mean I guess it just depends how you look at it. I mean obviously, yes. But, I mean, unless somebody's going to pay you just to be alive, which could be a good idea, but [laughs] unless you can totally do everything and make everything that you need, which is one of my goals [laughs], then yes, you have to work.

Is it hard to be happy in life?
Hard to be happy? Uh...I think it's hard to try to be happy, but I don't think it's hard—I don't know. No, it's not.

When was the last time that you saw me?
You know, I think it was three years ago or two years ago. I'm not sure.

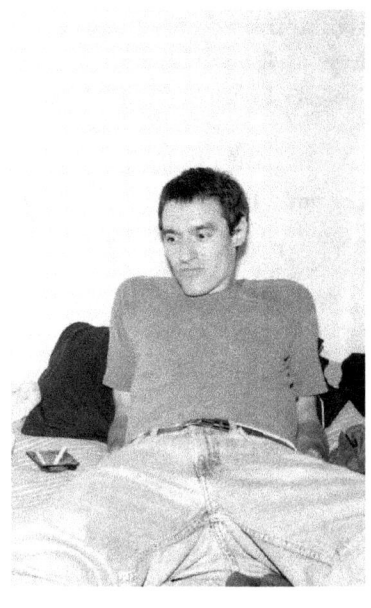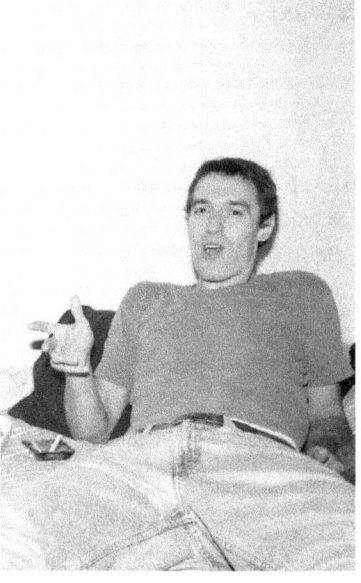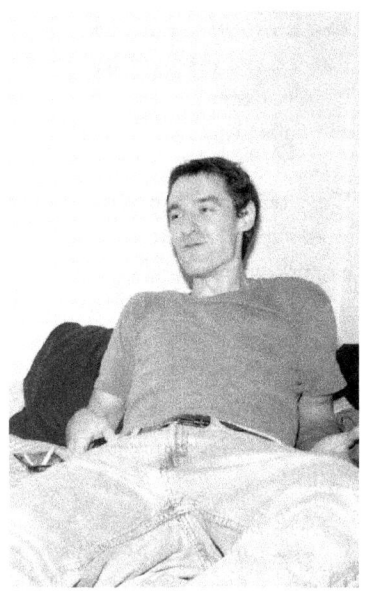

I interviewed Donald Mumford, my friend, in his apartment.

First off, wait, first off I want to protest at the presence of the tape recorder; as long as that's on the record I can go through with this.

How long have you known me?
Uh, let's see...it would be, uh...oh, man my arithmetic is bad [laughs]. It would be, uh, six and a half years—no, I'm sorry, seven and a half, seven and a half, right.

How much do I weigh?
You weigh about, uh...142, yeah.

What color are my eyes?
That's a bad one, you see—I'm really—I'd like to say that I've always been bad with eyes. OK, so that shouldn't be held against me. I shouldn't lose points for that. Um, I really can't say, they're like, um, are they brown? See, I have brown eyes so I think everyone has brown eyes [laughs].

How tall am I?
I'd say you're about, you're about five...five-seven, five-eight.

How well do you know me?
Oh now, come on, you see this is what I thought you were going to ask; and what do you mean by "know"?, like, Jim, how—do I know you? I've never known Jim in the biblical sense. I'd like to say that right now, OK.

You know some people better than others, and you have your own definition for "know," like I have my own definition for "know." In your judgement, how well do you know me?
I can't answer I—I, you know, I'm sorry, Jim, but I reject that question whenever I hear it from anyone, you know. In fact, I don't know how to—

How would you phrase that better; how would you phrase that to your liking?
[Exhalation.] No, it's like, um, it forces you to make this comparison, you know—it does, and, uh, you can't do that. See, and that's part of the free-love thing, you know. You're forced to, like—you're forced to meet everyone as sort of in isolation. It's really—that's the great thing about it. So, I can't use anyone else as a yardstick for you, you know. You're your only yardstick.

Would you say that you know me well?
Uh, now see you're forcing—I would say, alright, um, yeah, yeah, fairly well; I would say, I think, fairly well.

Would you say that you know me intimately?
Um...Goddamn, you know, I can't make this comparison. You're forcing me to rank you among everyone I know. You are, because I group everyone I know into these, like, categories, so I have to put you in there somewhere, right?

OK, wait, if you group everyone into categories, what category am I in?
That's—alright, that's what I'd have to, um, I guess, yeah; you know, that's how I'll remember you, as sort of being an intimate friend. You are, because you are sort of—well, you're my confidant regarding one area of my life. Although, I really can't delineate that area very well. You're not going to ask me to do that, are you? Good [laughs].

Do you remember being a little kid?
No.

What is your earliest memory?
Um, earliest...wow, that's hard because there are, like, a few of them. And some of them are so, like...you can't be sure if they're real.

Name several if that's better.
Um...earliest memory...I guess I, uh...I remember, uh, a peacock, a couple of peacocks. I think I lived near a peacock farm or something, um, back when I was trailer trash [laughs].

Do you remember being 20 years old?
Oh certainly, yeah! Oh hell, yeah!

Donald Mumford

Do you remember being 10 years old?

Uh, sure, yeah, yeah. I remember that year.

Do you like getting older?

Um, do I like getting older? Um, yeah, yeah I do. Well, I do and I don't. Sometimes it's really tough because I think I have a fundamentally nostalgic nature and, uh, it's just—even the bad stuff, you know, sometimes it's like I get this weird, I don't know, this weird high from it, from thinking about it. It is like— it is some sort of intoxicant, memory itself for me. Well, hell, I think everything is memory, really, you know...Am I answering the question?

Who do I most look like, my mother or my father?

Ah, really, you know, I've only seen a few pictures of each, I mean—I can't say. That's another one, that's like the eyes thing. I've never been good with that, like, uh, resemblances.

Would you guess of which do I share the most characteristics?

Uh, no, no, that doesn't interest me.

What is your earliest memory of me?

Uh, [laughs] I remember when you cut me off in, uh, you know that—I'm always reminding you of that—uh, the, um, Greek Philosophy. I was making a point [laughs].

Do you remember what that point was?

No, I don't. It was, um, I don't remember it. But it was important, I'm sure [laughs].

Can you name a few good qualities that I have?

No, this is corny—that's a corny question, I can't.

Phrase it how you would like.

Alright, um...yeah, I like you cause you're weird. I like you cause I never know what cornball project you're going to cook up next, you know [laughs], like this one [laughs].

Can you name a few bad qualities or weaknesses that I have?

Yeah, I think you're too afraid of sex, um, and anything even slightly erotic; um, what else? Oh, Aram and I talk about this all the time. Oh, maybe I shouldn't have said that [laughs]. I'd like that last remark to be stricken from the record, I don't even know an Aram.

This kind of relates to what—the first one, what I said before, that, uh, I don't think you like, um, the irrational. I don't think you value it, uh, enough. I think you need to be a lot more passionate and even aggressive; and, uh, something else, and this is sort related too, I think, uh—yeah, it is related, it is related. I think you need more, like, of a social courage. I think—you know we talked about that, uh, [David] Serlin scenario [laughs]. And you wouldn't tell your dining mate what you thought of—and I was like, I couldn't understand that. I was like, I would walk out of there that second. Should I recite that? Should we recite that for the—no.

Anything else?
I think you're way to hung up on, um, conventional norms of beauty, I think.

What in general are great qualities to have?
[Laughs.] That's a really corny one, come on.

What traits do you really admire in people that excite you? What are great traits?
I guess courage, uh, genuine altruism—and that's the trick knowing when it is genuine, you know, cause it's so easy to be slightly self-conscious about it, that kind of selflessness. Although I don't know. I don't happen to feel good about admiring that. There's also something about egoism that I kind of, I don't know. I guess what I'm trying to say is that I like ambiguity. That's probably my overarching value...ambiguity.

Who do you admire or find inspirational?
Well, I guess my heroes tend to be writers, um, just 'cause I think writing is kind of the most courageous act. That sounds kind of well, you know, not, not really—I mean obviously, like, putting your life on the line, that would be a more courageous act.

What writers?
Uh, I like Gide a lot. Should I, like, be like this? Should I be autobiographical like this? I guess so, I'm answering the question, what the hell. I like Gide just a lot because he, uh...he wrote a...sort of a, like, an early gay manifesto back in the '20s. He put his career on the line and, uh, I just think he has a great mind too. Um, who else? Uh...well, I admire what I think is genius.

Are people at base good or bad?
[Laughs.] Um...can I have one modify the other? Can they be goodly bad or badly good? [Laughs.] I can't say, I really can't answer that one. Sorry, ambiguity time again.

What are my hobbies?
Whatever it is you cook up, you know. This is it right now [laughs] I guess. Oh, wait you also, you—you're a cyclist too, an amateur cyclist, right? Aren't you? Wouldn't you say that is one of your hobbies? Oh, you can't agree or disagree, is that it? [Laughs.] But he's nodding his head [laughs].

Who are some of my close friends?
Um...Aram, um, Aram. Uh, you have friends from, I guess, that place you come from, what is it? What's the name of that place?

Levittown.
Yeah, that's it. That's the place that's famous for all the, um [laughs] the uniform housing, right, the tract housing, right—where conformity is such a value. Oh my God, it's like, uh, wait, [laughs] it's all clear now

[laughs].

Any other friends?

Any other close friends? Yeah, all those people, um, you know, that you talk about: your lawyer friend, Jackie, and, uh, Dave. I met them at a recent event.

What are some of my favorite things?

[Laughs.] If I were a better queer I could really put a sharp answer [laughs]. Uh, your favorite things? Um, you like a nice set of tits on a girl, I know. I know you really like that [laughs]. Uh, what else do you like? Um, you like it when you find those nifty anthologies, uh, in, you know, in used bookstores or on the street. You do have a knack for that.

　　　　Uh...would you repeat the question? [Question repeated.] Um, one could say something but I think my answer might fit a following question. Um, well I think you're, uh, I think you are very narcissistic. Does that really answer the question? Maybe—see, I thought maybe I should save that answer. Maybe I should have used that awhile ago when...but I wouldn't really know where to put it. It's just an observation, I wouldn't put it under good or bad or anything.

What are some of your favorite things?

I like, uh, I like, I like thinking about the openness of the future. I like thinking about that. Um...I like the idea of changing. Are these concrete, should I be answering it this way, favorite things? Do you mean, like, tangible things? I like a nice sunset. I like that, other than that I like, uh, what else? Let's see...can we go on?

Who is the most famous person you've met?

When I met Susan Sontag, yeah.

How many people are alive in the world?

What is it? Five billion now, five billion. Five and a half billion maybe now.

Are you convinced of God's existence?

[Laughs.] Next question [laughs]. God, that's like, "How well do you know me," you know, [laughs] come on. God, tsch.

Do you think you have free will?

Uh...no.

Why?

[Exhalation.] Well, I feel really bad that I can't quote Schopenhauer right now [laughs]. Um, because it's like what I said earlier, I think, you know, everything is memory and you're sort of shackled by that.

How many ideas of how to live, or what life is about, are your own?
Ah, that's impossible to answer.

Do you remember a time when I wasn't around?
[Laughs.] Uh, yeah. Yeah, I think I do [laughs]. My god, what do you think, I'm fried on drugs or something? [Laughs.]

Can you name some very important events in my life?
Uh...yeah! Yeah, of course I can, of course; uh, when you went to Europe; uh, that day you cut me off in Greek Philosophy [laughs]; the day you met Sue; um, I guess the day you got your degree, when you finally got it [laughs]. That's a joke, I'm the one who took 5 years to collect his diploma [laughs].

What most explains why I am like I am?
Um, fear.

Do I look different from when you first met me?
Um...yeah, I guess you do.

How so?
[Laughs.] Um, uh...you look softer. You look—you used to look mean, now you don't.

What is the dumbest thing I've done?
Um, dumbest thing? I did see you do something really dumb recently, but I don't remember what it was.

Can you name 3 very important events in your life?
Sure, yeah. Um...what was that—I'm sorry—was that again, what were they...

Three important events.
Oh, important. Um...when I got my own place, that was important. Uh...when I, uh, came out to my better friends, that was important. First time when I fooled around with a guy, that was important.

What most explains why you are like you are?
Uh, fear [laughs].

What would I consider some of my favorite places?
Uh, you seem to have a thing for museums...after that I really can't say.

What are some of your favorite places?
I don't know, I guess I sort of like the gothic motifs. Uh, you know, whatever that atmosphere, whenever I am around it. I like, uh, used bookstores. I think they're cool; I like the way they smell; I like the way they look; I like everything about them. Uh...I like, um, I like it when I, uh, I pick up a guy on the street and I

go back to his place knowing that I'll never be there again. I like that. Wherever it is, I like that place.

When was I probably most depressed?
Um, oh, that's easy, right after your break-up with Sue. Everybody knows that.

When was I probably most excited?
I don't know, I'd say a couple of times I guess vying for that, trying for—when you met, right after you met Sue I'm sure you were very—'cause nobody saw you. You guys were, like, always off doing something or behind your, you know, locked bedroom door for days on end [laughs]. But I guess, maybe, when you started at World Game, um...I don't know, I think we kind of, uh; I don't know how you feel about it but I thought some of that PIRG stuff we did in college was kind of fun, like Camp Baker. There was something cool about that, you know. It was kind of, I guess, a low-grade excitement but it was fun. I think we all had fun. [Laughs.] Remember that acting, remember that skit? Oh my god.

What would I consider my greatest achievements?
Your B.A. Uh...why a couple of your projects you were really, I think—some of them you seemed to feel just so-so about, but there were a couple I think you really liked.

When were you most depressed?
Um, most depressed...wow, I guess...most depressed...I guess, uh, if I have to be honest, I guess it was after, uh—well, I don't know if I'd call that depression. I was going to say after I broke up with Paul, um, things were really weird. But I—does that count, do you think? Yeah.

When were you most excited?
Uh, most excited...uh, I guess the first time I had sex, yeah.

What would I consider my biggest regrets?
Uh, heterosexuality [laughs]. Your biggest regrets, uh,...I don't know, I don't think you have any, like, uh, that you ever mentioned anything. That you didn't go to law school, yeah, that's it [laughs]. That was a joke [laughs].

What are your greatest achievements?
I don't know, I really can't—everything's really—I've been lucky. Everything's come easy, I mean, you know, everything [laughs]. I don't know, I've always been pretty happy and, uh, to be honest, I never felt like I worked for my happiness at all. Um, I really don't think I've suffered, uh, enough. Um...well, apart from that surgery, that was—wow—that was really...we won't go into details but that was painful, I suffered. Um, but aside from that...Am I answering the question?

What are your biggest regrets?
Well, you know, again because I, uh—it's hard for me to have regrets because nothing really bad has happened to me yet. Uh, my life has always had a neat little structure to it. Uh, sometimes I kick myself for

my laziness. I feel like—that I should have been working hard at something. But, you know, if you're not driven it just seems impossible to do. So, I really can't have any regrets.

What is some of my favorite music?
I guess you like Jazz, right? Don't you? I think you do. Um, you like anything that Woody Allen puts into one of his movies, yeah [laughs].

Can you name some of my dreams or goals?
Uh...no, I guess I can't really, like, specifically; I guess I'm not really sure what it is you want for yourself. I don't think you want the suburban thing—God, I hope not. Um, but...no, I can't, I can't say.

What are the most important things one can get out of living?
Um, just to do it...just to, uh, overcome fear, really. Just to live, you know, and to, uh, be a sensualist: Do what makes you feel good.

Is working an evil necessity?
Uh, yeah, yeah I guess so. Working, uh, yeah, as it is now [laughs], yeah, yeah it is.

Is it hard to be happy in life?
No, not at all!

Why not?
Uh, well, it's, um, it's a matter of being a realist...and not taking a lot of stuff for granted and, uh, enjoying the small things, you know, really. And by that I don't mean just surviving...maybe, I don't—maybe what I mean is just enjoying the good times, the good moments...'cause there ain't no rewind in life [laughs].

Donald Mumford

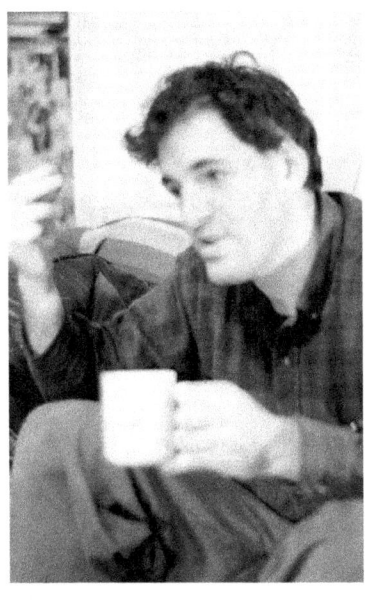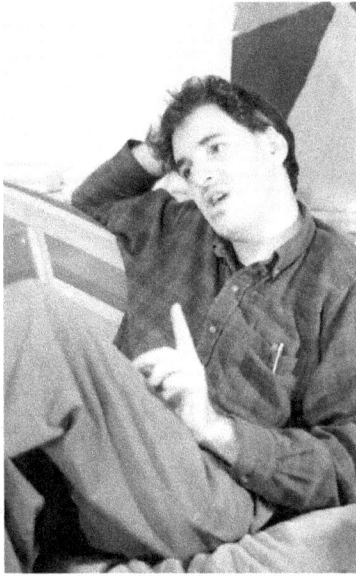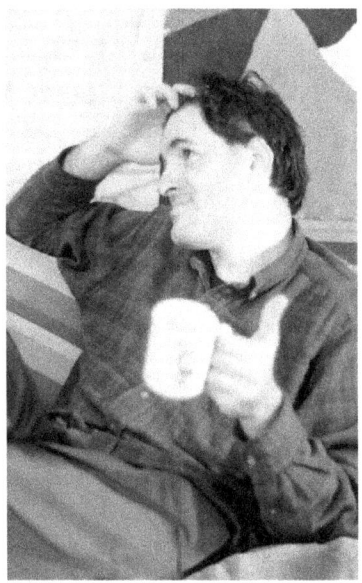

I interviewed Sherone Rabinovitz, my friend, in my apartment.

How long have you known me?
I've known you, um, guess five years? Five years.

How much do I weigh?
You weigh, uh, probably around, between 130 and 140. I have no idea.

What color are my eyes?
A sort of brown, kind of a hazel-kind-of-brown.

How tall am I?
Five foot four.

How well do you know me?
I think I know you...pretty damn well [laughs]. I think.

Do you remember being a little kid?
Yes.

What is your earliest memory?
I remember falling in the sandbox in kindergarten, cutting my forehead, having to get stitches. I remember my dad. I remember being at my Grandma's house and my other grandparents' house in Jerusalem. So I think that would be either four or five years old. That's about some of the earliest—I mean, that's the age

of some of my earliest memories. I can tell you that much.

Do you remember being 20 years old?
Yeah, I guess so. Um, yeah.

Ten?
Yeah.

Do you like getting older?
It's OK. It's got a good beat, you can dance to it [laughs]. It's...yeah, sometimes. Not always though.

Who do I most look like, my mother or my father?
Having never met your father, and seen a picture of him once, I would say you look like Abraham Lincoln. Um, I really don't know. Uh, I guess—I don't know.

Of which do I share the most characteristics?
I'd say your father.

What is your earliest memory of me?
I think the night I met you. Probably at Gina's party—birthday party—on Rodman Street. You went between two parties all night.

Can you name a few good qualities that I have?
You are honest, yet deceptive [laughs]. Um...I think you're fair, you're diplomatic, you're rational. You wouldn't make a rash emotional decision, at least you rarely do that. I think you are responsible; maybe not when it comes to affairs that have to do with yourself, but at least in dealing with other people. You're down to earth. You're curious, you're funny, absolutely amazing in bed, but that's hearsay. Is that enough? That's a few characteristics.

Can you name a few bad qualities or weaknesses that I have?
Yeah. There's probably...vanity—stop smiling—[laughs] more than somebody as bright as you should have, I would say. Um...fear of failure, but that's something so many of us share. But you're cautious...too much so. I mean, there's a part that's perfectionist, but there's also a part that's just...just too cautious; like things will take too long. It's like you have to cover your ass completely and entirely. You should jump into the flame sometime. I think that's a few off the top of my head.

What in general are great qualities to have?
Let's see...in general. Well, honesty is very important; being down to earth; being industrious; being spiritual but also being practical...have to be a good mix; a sense of humor is very important; to be emotional; to be inspired.

Who do you admire or find inspirational?

Michael Jordan [laughs]. I don't know if he's a direct inspiration, but it's just somebody I really admire. As far as inspiration, I don't know. I just don't know anymore—lots of people, I guess, tons. But he's just somebody I really, really respect.

Are people at base good or bad?

They're good.

What are my hobbies?

Um, sex if you'd have more of it. Your hobbies are arts in all its forms: music—I don't think literary is as high on your list as the others—sports, basketball, projects! I guess that goes into the art thing. Just learning, just movement of the mental type—intellectual curiosity.

Who are some of my close friends?

Well, Don, Aram, Jack, I guess myself—are you supposed to include yourself? Those are some of the top people. There's other people but, I know, I don't know how close you are with them.

What are some of my favorite things?

Are you talking about objects, items, or hobbies or things to do?

It's pretty much open to what you believe.

I think being with really cool people, people that share some of the same...lust for life that you have [laughs]. Those are definitely some of your favorite things. Woody Allen movies are some of your favorite things; discussions; philosophy; learning; sports. It kind of overlaps with the hobbies. But I'd have to say being with really good people—just being with people in general, you really like that.

What are some of your favorite things?

Some of my favorite things are chocolates, music, women—beautiful women with really cool personalities and wonderful nipples. God, so many things, tons of things: Art, sports, travel and just being with people who are exciting, inspiring, interesting.

Who is the most famous person you've met?

I met Charles Barkley once, but do you mean a casual meeting or just...

It's open.

I met a bunch of people working at the Chart House but they were kind of sports figures. That might be it, I don't know. I might get back to you on that.

How many people are alive in the world?

About 5 billion.

Are you convinced of God's existence?

That's a tricky one because you get into all these definitions of what God is—not of what existence is but just what God is—I'm convinced in some higher power; whether it's just weird energy source or an actual entity that's all-knowing, and all-doing, and all-powerful and all those omni-words. I don't know but...

Do you think you have free will?

Yes.

How do you deal with that?

I don't know that I do. I just...I don't think about it. I don't think it is anything to be dealt with. I just kind of try to do what it is that I want to do. Not that I succeed all the time. But I, you know...

How many ideas of how to live, or what life is about, are your own?

Well...I guess the bottom line is *none* because you're fed all this stuff anyway. And then you kind of discriminate and distinguish; and you heard some of it and you keep some of it and *modify* some of it and custommake it to yourself. But the thing you are modifying to begin with is probably not yours. It's stuff that you read, stuff that other people talked to you about, stuff that you learned. So none of it really. I guess it is how you look at it. It is mine, it is something I worked out for myself and it's something I'm constantly trying to—I'm constantly deliberating that idea. But the source is all from other people really.

Do you remember a time when I wasn't around?

Yes I do, Jim. One of my favorite times, really.

Can you name 3 important events in my life?

Sure. Probably when your parents got separated, be it physically or emotionally. I guess they are both separate but I guess we can hook them into one. Important events in your life: going to Europe! I'd say that was pretty important. And the whole Suerella [Sue Lerch] thing. I don't know if that counts as an event but...

Could you say what you mean by that?

Well, the relationship. I guess you never really know how long it would last when it started, or how profound it would be. So I can't name the event of your meeting her as that. But I'd say when you moved in together that was probably a big, big move. I'd say when you first separated but then you went after her. I remember you were going to, I don't know if you did or didn't, but you were—I think you did—you were going to have flowers delivered while you were having dinner somewhere to try to win her back or something. The day that, I guess, you separated again, that would be another one. That's what I mean, the Suerella thing. That whole relationship.

What most explains why I am like I am?

Your early childhood [laughs]. Is that too generic?

Sherone Rabinovitz

Do I look different from when you first met me?
Probably.

Can you be specific?
Yes. You probably lost some hair, how's that? You matured, I guess, physically. You're more of a "man," whatever that means, than you are when you were twenty-five.

What is the dumbest thing I've done?
The dumbest thing you've done, besides this interview is, uh [laughs]. The dumbest thing you've done? God, I don't know...the dumbest thing you've done: taking so long to quit that job as a bike messenger [laughs]. I have to qualify that answer by saying that I don't really know.

Can you name 3 important events in your life?
When my father was killed, when we moved to the United States, and...I guess the whole music project, which can be divided into actually going to the studio and recording it, and thereby performing it in front of at least one other live, stranger, person. Then having it play on the radio—twice. It's pretty important stuff.

What most explains why you are like you are?
The same thing that does you, early childhood experiences.

What do you think I consider some of my favorite places?
I'd say the basketball court was one of them. I mean there is the general and the specific. I'd say any basketball court could be one of your favorite places. I'd say a good museum could be one of your favorite places. I'd say...New York. But that's kind of, I'm not sure about that. I'd say your own place, where you feel comfortable, where you have your things, where you have your space, your time and your music. Those are some of your favorite places.

What are some of your favorite places?
One of my favorite places is a specific place—is in the north of Israel. It's right on the border with Lebanon and it's mountainous. It's on the ocean, there is a lot of tunnels. It's very beautiful. That's a favorite place. And other places are, they're kind of more defined by the people or the events that are taking place. One of my favorite places is being with my guitar and my amplifier—anywhere really. But it's my space, it's my time if there's nobody around. I like being on the computer too for that kind of reason; places where I can be creative, where I can think freely and just kind of be myself.

When was I most depressed?
When you broke up with Sue, or she broke up with you, or whatever.

When was I most excited?
It could be you were most excited when you were with a loved one. It could be sex; it could be a love-

making type of a thing. I don't know. I think in a way maybe some of your most exciting moments are ahead of you.

When were you most depressed?
Probably some of those months during the time that I was going—when I was in therapy and trying to deal with my father's death. That's when I was most consciously depressed. I may have been way depressed before that, but I certainly wasn't aware of it, or I wasn't dealing with it.

When were you most excited?
I don't know. I was definitely excited to hear my song on the radio, but I wouldn't even say that was the most exciting part. I was excited...with some of the girls that I've been with and I've really liked. It's just exciting to be around them. Excited every time a plane took off and I knew I was going to travel some place. Excited...I don't know, sometimes you just hear a piece of music on the radio, like your favorite song, you know it's going to play; you know it's going to be number one on the chart. It's really exciting. Or I bring a new piece of music that I love and I get to know its chords so now I can sit down and play it. It's exciting as hell. Things like that. It kind of varies. But I can be very excited about various things to a similar degree.

What do you think I consider my greatest achievements?
Going to Europe is one of them...I know I should know more. You know, going to Europe I think definitely was one of them. Some of the other ones I'm not sure about. I'm tempted to say that riding on your bike to the shore would have been one of them, but I know it's not. Like maybe it should have been, but it isn't. I know that you don't let on a lot of times what it is that really...moves you. So I don't know. But once again I'd have to say that, uh, your greatest achievements are ahead of you.

What would I consider my biggest regrets?
There's probably a whole bunch of girls that you should have asked out, not to mention bagged. Just...I don't know specifics necessarily, but just taking chances overall. Or what you would consider to be taking chances. Trying to overcome your fears.

What do you consider your greatest achievements?
Well, I got an erection and, uh, [laughs]. Years of scientific testing there...Um, greatest achievements? The whole music thing but a lot of these—I guess this goes for you too—a lot of them, as soon as you achieve it, well, well that was nothing, you know. It kind of shrinks because there's so much more you can do now. Sometimes I think it's been a great achievement to have stayed sane and spiritually alive and inspired in the face of some of the things I've had to deal with, meaning the family circumstances, moving and all this traumatic shit, and not being a drug addict or alcoholic, whatever. Or anything like that. I'd say they're still ahead of me though.

What do you consider your biggest regrets?
I don't know if it's—does regret mean something that you wanted to do but didn't do, or just something

Sherone Rabinovitz

Sherone Rabinovitz

you feel sorry you weren't able to experience?

I think it means both.

Because I wish I knew my father more. I regret not having known him. But that doesn't really have to do with me. Sometimes I wish we hadn't moved to the United States. But I still feel there's probably a lot of good that came out of it and it's up to me to make the best out of it. It's not a good attitude to just regret it. It can also be celebrated.

What is some of my favorite music?

Jim likes crooners: Frank Sinatra, Tony Bennett, those guys—Mel Tormé. Jim likes Rap, Hip-House— Hip-House—I mean Hip-Hop. His own stuff. Jim likes Led Zeppelin big time. Those are the 3 major very different categories...and The B-52s.

Can you name some of my dreams or goals?

I'd say to make a name for himself somehow. To be in some kind of position of power. To do something artistic, something expressive. I mean probably to achieve these positions of status or power through doing something artistic, expressive. That kind of a thing. To be—not to be a household name—but to be...to be a respectable, a respected person, individual. If you want specifics, it would probably have to do with... it could do with cinema, or music, or comedy. A combination somehow of all these things combined. Something along those lines.

What are the most important things one can get out of living?

A good cheesesteak. The more important things you can get out living? And you can't specify that any-more?

I'm afraid I can't.

Self-fulfillment, self-actualization and knowledge that you've done everything the right way, or in a morally correct way. Which is very ambiguous I know but...I think it's understood what I mean. But, you know, self-fulfillment, self-actualization type of things.

Is working an evil necessity?

There's a couple of terms we can define here: what working means, what necessity is? Sometimes, not always. Working to me means something you're doing where you're not really enjoying it and you're not... Working means you'd rather be doing something else and it is an evil necessity—Yes! In the sense that you need to do it because you need to have money. First of all, to live, but hopefully to fund the things that you really want to be doing. So sometimes you have to do that. I don't feel I'm the right person to ask that question [laughs].

But if working is not enjoyable what would you call it then? If working is something you don't want to do. Is there a term for something that you want to do that isn't the word "working?"

Yeah, living [laughs]. If you do for a living—if you earn your money doing something you love—I don't think you're working. I mean I'll be the first one to say that it can be very taxing, it can be a lot of hard work; it could be exhausting. It often is when something is close to you and dear to your heart. It will take much more out of you than some menial labor type of activity. But it's not working. I wouldn't see it as working.

Is it hard to be happy in life?
For some people, yes; for some people, no. Yes! I think...I can only answer that for myself. For me, right now, yes. If you don't have love, it is very hard. If you have love it makes a lot of things much easier.

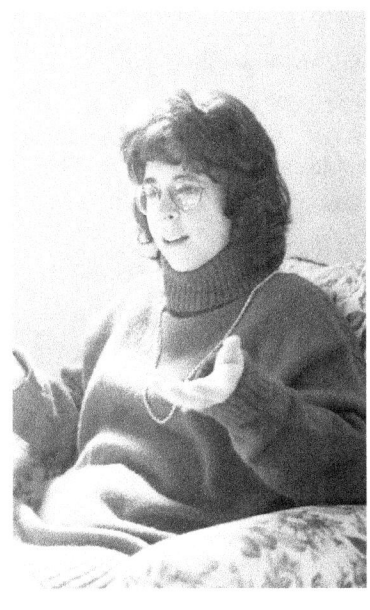 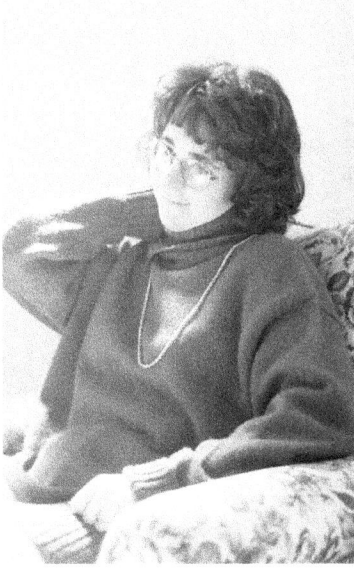 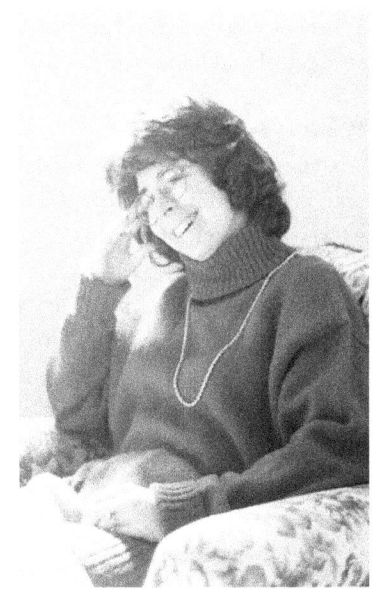

I interviewed Julie Rita, my sister, in her house.

How long have you known me?
Twenty-eight years.

How much do I weigh?
145.

What color are my eyes?
Hazel.

How tall am I?
Five-seven.

How well do you know me?
I don't know, how well does anybody know anybody? Um, I don't know, mediocre I guess. I don't know.

But you know some people pretty well?
Yeah, I know some people pretty well.

Do you remember being a little kid?
Yes.

What is your earliest memory?
A dream I had when, um, I think I was under the age of three—I was definitely under the age of three.

What was the dream?
[Exhalation.] I had a dream that I was laying in bed and these little elf people came into my room. They marched up, took my teddy bear, pulled off his eye and then stuck the teddy bear in the closet and then walked out. That's my earliest memory. Well, that's not really a memory, that's a dream, so...

How do you know you were under three?
Because my parents were still together, we lived on Bolton Lane.

Do you remember being 20 years old?
Vaguely.

Do you remember being 10 years old?
Not especially.

Do you like getting older?
It doesn't bother me so much.

Who do I most look like, my mother or my father?
Mother.

Of which do I share the most characteristics?
Ooh, that's hard. It depends, it's split, I think. I think it's pretty evenly split; it depends. If you're talking... communication skills and physical gestures, then you're more like dad, if you're talking ideology and ways of thinking, then you're more like mom. That's why I say it's split.

What is your earliest memory of me?
My earliest memory of you? I don't know...I don't know, I would pause it because it is going to take me awhile to think of this. [Pause.] Now it's really vague, but the earliest memory I can think of was a party that mom and dad had and the kids weren't allowed to go to the party, so we had to stay in the bedroom and I remember some other kids there. I'm pretty sure you were there, I think you had to be because if I was there you would have been there. And all we could do was stay in this room and then somebody brought us in some food, some, like, potato chips or jelly beans or something. And that is my earliest memory.

How old do you think you were?
[Exhalation.] Three.

Can you name a few good qualities that I have?
Logical, um, fair...analytical.

Can you name a few bad qualities or weaknesses that I have?
Procrastinate, um...tend to get angry when you argue, um...what else?...I don't know.

What in general are great qualities to have?
Kindness, caring, honesty, um, a general concern for people.

Who do you admire or find inspirational?
Um...Martin Luther King, um...Jesus, the disciples.

Are people at base good or bad?
I like to think they're good.

What are my hobbies?
Reading, art, photography.

Who are some of my close friends?
Um, Doug, Paul—Jack, Jack—I always call him Paul, Aram.

What are some of my favorite things?
Woody Allen, books about Woody Allen, anything by Woody Allen, his movies, [exhalation] books on art, Art, literature.

What are some of your favorite things?
Um...like specific items?

It doesn't have to be
I don't know. My favorite things, I don't know, like, my house, pretty much, my dog, but I don't have more than one dog so you can't really have a favorite, um, I don't know.

Who is the most famous person you've met?
Most famous person I have met? Um...Peter Kostmayer, he used to be a Congressman for Bucks County.

How many people are alive in the world?
Two or five billion.

Are you convinced of God's existence?
Yes.

Do you think you have free will?
Yes.

How do you deal with that?
The fact that you have free will in relation to God, or just that you have free will?

Just that you have free will.
There's not really much to deal with: you have it, you just don't abuse it. You got to live within the reins of certain things: morality.

How many ideas of how to live, or what life is about, are your own?
Meaning completely thought up on my own?

Yes.
Well, I think, basically, all my thoughts, eh, are influenced by something else, by something I read, by something I hear. So I wouldn't say that any of them are generated specifically within myself.

Do you remember a time when I wasn't around?
Um, yeah, when you were away at college.

Can you name 3 very important events in my life?
[Exhalation.] I would assume the [parents'] divorce, um...going to college and going to Europe.

What most explains why I am like I am?
Um...the way you were brought up, I guess, and, uh, given the freedom to develop your own ideas and thoughts and individuality without a lot of rigidity about what you should or shouldn't be.

Do I look different from when you first met me?
Uh, yeah [laughs] because when I first met you you were a kid. You look a lot different.

How specifically do I look different?
Well, you're grown, you're an adult. Obviously your features have changed since you were a baby or a very young child.

What is the dumbest thing I've done?
Um, get lost coming back from Oxford Valley Mall.

Can you name 3 very important events in your life?
Um, my wedding; um, going to college at Umass [University of Massachusetts]...and the divorce. That's three events.

Julie Rita

What divorce?
Parents' divorce.

What most explains why you are like you are?
Um, the church.

What would I consider some of my favorite places?
Philadelphia, New York City, um, is that good enough?

What are some of your favorite places?
Um, Massachusetts, specifically, western Mass.; um, Bucks County, upper Bucks specifically, um, that's it.

When was I probably most depressed?
Hmm...I don't know.

When was I probably most excited?
Before you went to Europe.

When were you most depressed?
Um, high school.

When were you most excited?
Um, I think it varies, marriage to Ron.

What would I consider my greatest achievements?
Graduating college, going to Europe.

What would I consider my biggest regrets?
Do I have to name specific examples?

If you would like.
Ah, I don't know specific examples, but I would assume that, [exhalation] that there was a time when you didn't do something and you wished you would have, like, maybe something happened in high school and you regret not doing it or you regret doing it, um, but I can't name specifics.

What are your greatest achievements?
Graduating college and, uh, going to Europe and, uh, having a happy marriage.

What are your biggest regrets?
Hmm. Biggest regrets: the way I led my life during my high school years and, uh, not being more outgoing.

What is some of my favorite music?

I don't know. Wha—I don't say New Age, but the more...something along the lines of B-52s, maybe, or the newer music that's out but I don't know what it's called. I guess it is pretty eclectic.

Can you name some of my dreams or goals?

Um...no.

What are the most important things one can get out of living?

Well, if there is a purpose I think it comes from the relationships that you build with people and, uh...um, that's it.

Is working an evil necessity?

No, not necessarily, no. It's necessary but it's not necessarily evil.

Is it hard to be happy in life?

No, very simple, very easy.

Julie Rita

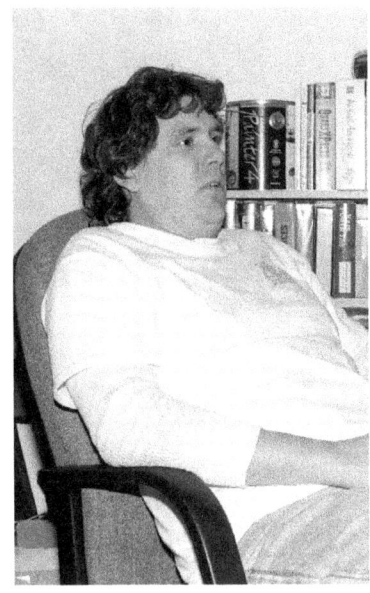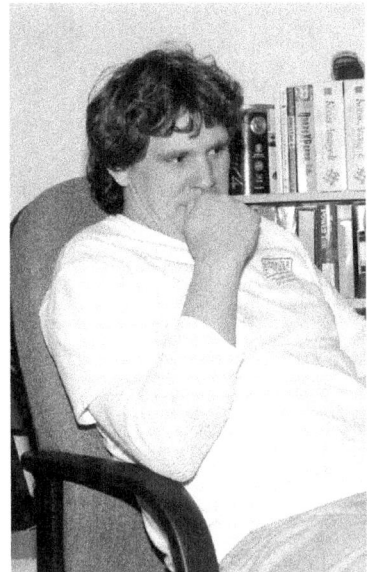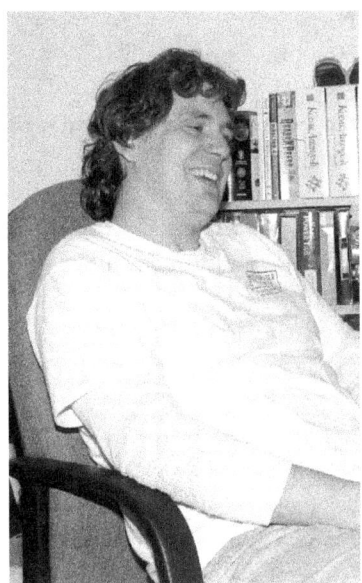

I interviewed David G. Roberts, my friend, four times to ask all of these questions. The first time he was driving us somewhere. The other times we were in his house.

How long have you known me?
I don't know...six years, eight years, five years? Since, since...uh, since 1985.

How much do I weigh?
[Laughs.] Um, 147 pounds.

What color are my eyes?
Brown.

How tall am I?
I know that answer already. Um, you're four-eleven and three-quarters.

Is that a serious answer?
Um...[pause] yeah. I guess—yeah! That's about five foot. I'm six, you could be five with no problem. Five feet something.

How well do you know me?
Is it a scale?

No.
How about pretty well.

Do you remember being a little kid?
Yes.

What is your earliest memory?
My earliest memory is pre-school that I can date.

Anything specific?
Playing with blocks in the pre-school classroom.

Do you remember being 10 years old?
I don't know how old that was.

Do you like getting older?
Uh, sh—yes.

Who do I most look like, my mother or my father?
Father.

Of which do I share the most characteristics?
Most characteristics...personality or physical?

Personality.
I don't know your father that well so it's kind of hard to say. I'd say it'd be a pretty good fifty-fifty split.

What is your earliest memory of me?
Hmm. A very brief encounter when I first went over to see Julie [my sister].

Can you name a few good qualities that I have?
Good temperament, um...common sense...um, and outgoing.

Can you name a few bad qualities or weaknesses that I have?
Yes. The indecisiveness has got to be biggest downfall...and...that's it.

What in general are great qualities to have?
Courteous, kind, obedient, thrifty, brave, clean and reverent.

Who do you admire or find inspirational?
This week? Inspirational...[pause] it changes every week. It depends on what I'm into this week, or this

David G. Roberts

month. So, next question.

Are people at base good or bad?
Hmm. Well, after having this discussion with Mark, my pastor friend, uh, I think people are right now more on the bad side.

What are my hobbies?
Jim, your hobbies would be skiing, high impact aerobics...and withdrawing books from the library for long periods of time.

Who are some of my close friends?
I have no idea.

Oh, come on, I know you know.
I don't remember their names: Phil, Bob and Marsha, something like that.

No answer?
No answer.

What are some of my favorite things?
Your favorite things? Like sex? Old Jaguar S class, J class, something like that. And, um, pasta.

What are some of your favorite things?
Seafood. An abundance of money that I can spell without remorse—spell or spend. And...well-built, well-made things.

Who is the most famous person you've met?
I don't even know his name and it wasn't anybody to even worry about anyway.

How many people are alive in the world?
How many people? Like 40 million, 42.3 billion people?

Are you convinced of God's existence?
No.

Do you think you have free will?
Yes.

How do you deal with that?
Um, I don't worry about it.

How many ideas of how to live, or what life is about, are your own?
Well...probably all of them, because I don't know the terms and names of everybody else.

Do you remember a time when I wasn't around?
Yes.

Can you name 3 important events in my life?
Um, OK. Your parents' separation, your graduating from college, and, um, your moving out of your house into the city.

What most explains why I am like I am?
Your parents' separation. Out of those events, right?

No, anything.
Oh, well, well, jees. It's not very explicit.

Do I look different from when you first met me?
Yes.

Anyway specific?
You were thinner then.

What is the dumbest thing I've done?
[Laughs.] Too many of them to name.

Name some.
Um, your tire deal [fell off car while driving.] The lack of direction when you went—tried to get to the [Oxford Valley] mall and you ended up in New Hope. Um, those are, those are pretty much tops.

What are some of your favorite places?
My most favorite place is under—at the bottom of the refrigerator door where the heat comes out of the bottom of the grate.

Any other places?
Nope. Just one answer is fine.

What would I consider some of my favorite places?
[Pause.] New York.

When was I probably most depressed?
[Laughs.] I don't know that one.

David G. Roberts

When was I probably most excited?
When you were dating Sue.

When were you most depressed?
Uh, I don't know that.

When were you most excited?
Um, when I was dating Sue.

What would I consider my greatest achievements?
Yours, what would you consider yours? Graduating college.

Is that it?
Yes.

What would I consider my biggest regrets?
Hmm...I don't know.

What are your greatest achievements?
The questions are worded awfully similar. What was three above it?

I said what would I consider my greatest achievements, now I'm asking what are your greatest achievements.
Hmm...I think owning my house is pretty exciting. I like it. I'm into that.

What are your biggest regrets?
Hmm...I don't know. Next.

What is some of my favorite music?
[Laughs.] How do I know? B-52s.

Can you name some of my dreams or goals?
No.

What are the most important things one can get out of living?
How about just the chance to explore and experience things for themselves.

Is working an evil necessity?
No.

Why?
Because it's fun.

Is it hard to be happy in life?
No.

Why?
Because it's not hard.

Do you remember being 20 years old?
Sure.

Do you remember being 10 years old?
Sure.

What most explains why you are like you are?
Parents...way I was brought up.

The "way you were brought up"?
Where, why, how.

Can you name 3 very important events in your life?
Um...[pause] buying my house, my mom's cancer and John McBride's Cream of Mushroom soup.

Why John McBride's Cream of Mushroom Soup?
I'm not telling you.

David G. Roberts

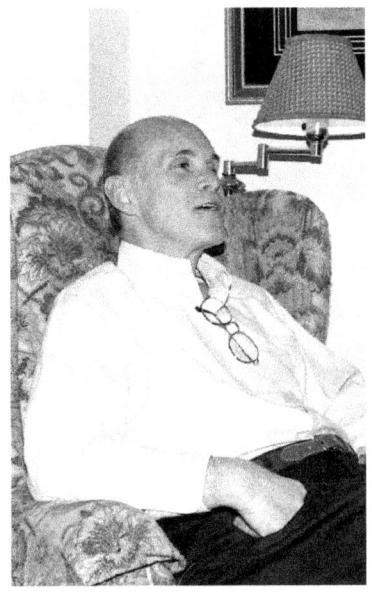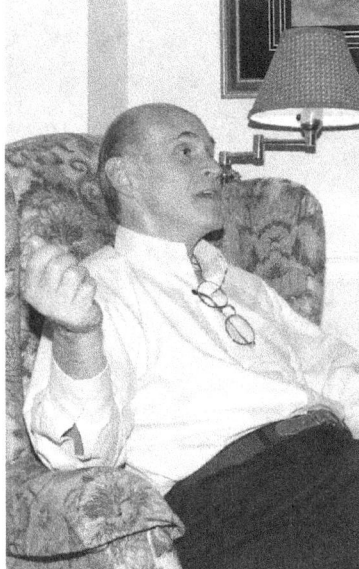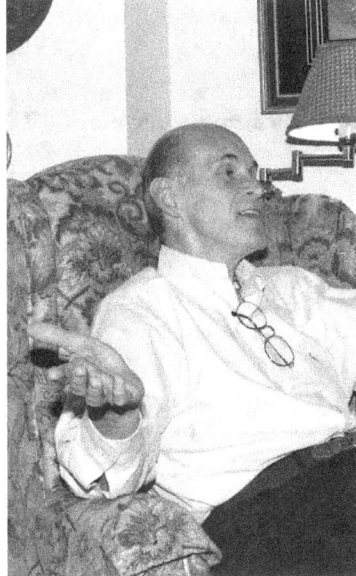

I interviewed James K. Tantum, Sr., my father, twice with both times in his house.

How long have you known me?
However old you are. I believe you're thirty, or will be thirty.

How much do I weigh?
I don't have any idea. I'd say 140 pounds.

What color are my eyes?
Brown.

How tall am I?
Five-five.

Do you remember being a little kid?
Ah, occasionally.

What is your earliest memory?
I'll have to think about that...my earliest memory, I don't remember how old I was, I was dressed up in a cowboy suit, wearing a silly hat, and somebody took my picture.

Do you remember being 20 years old?
Not specifically, no.

Around that age though?
No. Yes, yes I do.

Do you remember being 10 years old?
Yes.

Do you like getting older?
No.

Who do I most look like, you or my mother?
Your mother.

Of which do I share the most characteristics?
I believe you emulate me more than your mother.

What is your earliest memory of me?
When you were born [laughs].

Can you name a few good qualities that I have?
No.

Can you name a few bad qualities or weaknesses that I have?
Yes. You procrastinate.

Anything else?
No.

What in general are five great qualities to have?
Ambition, perspicacity, focus, sensitivity, respect.

Who do you most admire or find inspirational?
Winston Churchill.

Are people at bottom good or bad?
What do you mean by "bottom"?

Very basically.
I don't know what that means.

The common denominator: are people generally good or generally bad?
Generally good.

What are my hobbies?
Reading, bicycle riding, photography.

Can you name some of my close friends?
No. Well, yes, one, David somebody.

What are some of my favorite things?
Oatmeal.

What are some of your favorite things?
Uh, Brooks Brothers, filet mignon, Polo, driving, Short Hills Mall, Joe's American Bar & Grill.

Who is the most famous person you've met?
Uh...some actor.

How many people are alive in the world?
Billions, I'm not sure how many.

Are you convinced of God's existence?
No.

Do you think you have free will?
Yes.

How do you deal with that?
I exert it.

How many ideas of how to live, or what life is about, are your own?
Probably none.

Do you remember a time when I wasn't around?
Yes.

Can you name 3 important events in my life?
College graduation, acceptance in college, high school graduation.

What most explains why I am like I am?
DNA, RNA.

Do I look different from when you first met me?
[Laughs.] Yes.

What is the dumbest thing I've done?

Not knowing when to exit Route 95. Continuing to drive until you ran out of gas. And not calling anybody.

What would I consider some of my favorite places?

I don't know.

When was I probably most depressed?

I don't know.

When was I probably most excited?

I don't know.

What do you think I consider my greatest achievement?

I'm not sure, you've never told me.

What do you think I consider my biggest regret?

I don't know.

What is some of my favorite music?

B-52, uh...Dave Brubeck, and that, uh, esoteric group that I had to buy for Christmas that nobody ever heard of.

Can you name some of my dreams or goals?

Have a photography exhibit, become a photographer...uh, not have to work.

What are some of your favorite places?

Philadelphia, Boston, Grand Canyon, San Francisco, San Diego...and, uh, and Phoenix, Arizona and Sedona, Arizona; London, England; Nice, France.

When were you most depressed?

When I got divorced.

When were you most excited?

I don't know.

You can name several things.

Several things. I think when I, when I first had a drive in a Jaguar. I think when I got laid the first time, had sex the first time. Uh...and I think...I don't know. That's about it.

James K. Tantum, Sr.

Can you name 3 very important events in your life?

Uh...graduating from high school, that's pretty important; graduating from college, that was important, I think, although not as important as, uh, getting married—I got married. Birth of the children was important. That's four things.

What most explains why you are like you are?

I don't know. Being an only child, I think—or almost an only child. My sister was so much older than I was. It was like being an only child and I was spoiled, I think.

What are your greatest achievements?

Greatest achievements? I think, uh, finally getting through graduate school will be...an achievement. I think that's it.

What are your biggest regrets?

Biggest regrets? I don't think I have any regrets.

Is working an evil necessity?

No. I enjoy work.

Is it hard to be happy in life?

I think you have to work at it, but I don't think it's hard. I think you have to have an optimistic outlook.

What are the most important things one can get out of living?

Achieving all the things that I just mentioned.

When you remember me as a little kid, do you miss that little child?

No.

What did he lose as he aged?

Innocence...dependence.

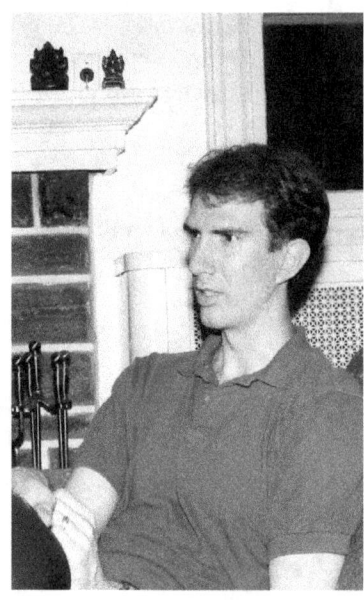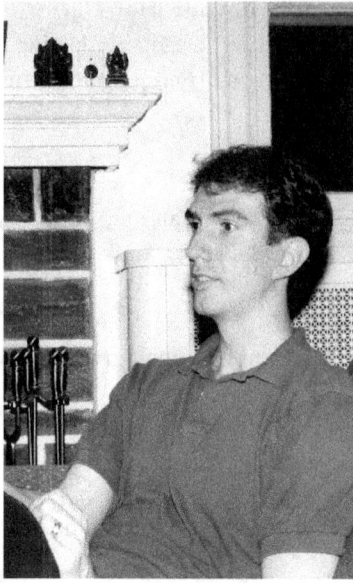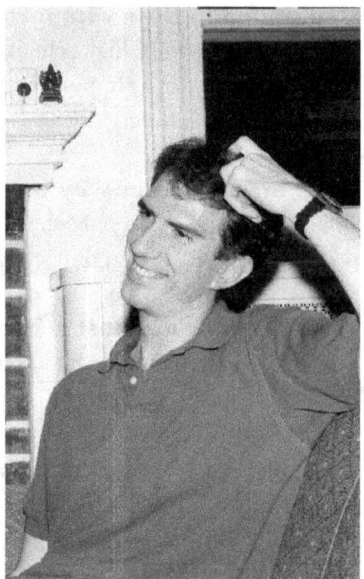

I interviewed Doug Wilson, my friend, in his house.

How long have you known me?
Testing my memory, let me see...I'm going to guess...wow!, a long time. I'm going to guess, uh...eighteen years.

How much do I weigh?
You weigh one hundred and...fifty-eight pounds. No, you weigh one hundred, yeah, 158.

What color are my eyes?
Brown.

How tall am I?
You are five-four.

How well do you know me?
Pretty well, um, pretty well.

Do you remember being a little kid?
Can I ask for clarification? What do you mean by a "little kid?"

A young child.
The youngest—the earliest memory I have that I can remember clearly that I knew exactly what age I

84

was, looking back on it, is when I was four. Otherwise, I pretty much remember, like, from maybe seven on.

What is your earliest memory?
My earliest memory was when my brother turned ten which was in 1970, so I was four years old.

Do you remember being 20 years old?
I don't remember any...um, I mean I can if I think back. I can remember what year of college I was in when I was twenty and remember where I lived and what classes I took and who I knew. So, yeah. I'd have to mentally do that.

Do you remember being 10 years old?
Yes.

Do you like getting older?
Um, I don't necessarily like my age increasing. I definitely like the experiences associated with, you know, the progress of life, such as having a family.

Who do I most look like, my mother or my father?
Um, I haven't seen your father too many times. I'd have to say your mom, especially with your hair the way it is now.

Of which do I share the most characteristics?
Um...I'd have to say—it's very difficult for me to say. I basically don't know your father very well, but even that being the case I will say your father.

What is your earliest memory of me?
My earliest memory would be in Sunday school classes just kind of sitting around the table reading from our books, writing things.

Can you name a few good qualities that I have?
A few good qualities. You have a very good sense of humor, you are very honest, um...and that, you know, I don't think you have any kind of, for lack of a better expression, any hidden agendas. I think you are who you are. And, you know, you always get a straight answer with questions, feelings, things like that. Um, I think you're a lot of fun, you know, which might go along with the sense of humor, but, you know, somewhat adventurous; um, nice to talk to, always can...offer some kind of an opinion, or suggestion, or thoughts on a lot of different topics, so always nice to talk to; um...that's a few [laughs.] Is that a few?

Can you name a few bad qualities or weaknesses that I have?
Um...yeah, I'm sure there are, uh...[Pause.] OK...weaknesses or bad qualities I think was the question and one thing I guess I can think of is that I think, um—and I said one of the good qualities I think I men-

tioned was honesty, um...which I think is a good quality and—but I think sometimes, um...there's etiquette or "white lies" that could be used which aren't sometimes. Um, so I guess the term "painfully honest"— that could be applied, I don't know. Although, I can't, you know, I probably can't give you any examples; I think sometimes there's inconsistencies in philosophy...and I'll go with that.

What in general are great qualities to have?

For anybody? Um, well...sense of humor, honesty [chuckle]; um, someone I guess who can think of, or be cognizant of, someone else's feelings and, you know, be a very real and caring person, and be able to put yourself in someone else's position and understand what someone else is thinking about or feeling or going through. Um...you know, I guess, being yourself, not trying to put up a front too much.

Who do you admire or find inspirational?

Uh, I admire my family as a whole; um, I think I have always kind of admired my brother, Steve, quite a bit—I still do. I admire everybody in my family, but I guess I would pick him out a little bit more than the others, maybe. Um, through my career there's been a few people that I have admired and really as far as career in the workplace there really hasn't been—I really never had a mentor in that respect. As far as someone famous, you know, like a...any politicians or do-gooders or people like that, I really don't have anybody in particular that I would think of that would hold any importance on how I go through life.

Are people at base good or bad?

What do you mean "at base"?

Taken as a whole, overall, are people just in their heart just good or bad?

That's a very interesting question, you know, what good or bad is but I guess we can talk about that a little bit. Um...I would have to say that, well, I think when you're born, you know, I think it is basically a clean slate and how you are in your life and how you're raised and how your family raises you. There's always, I think—part of being a human being is being competitive and always wanting to out do somebody else and that can always—and greed, you know, things like that, those things that can be looked at as bad or good—maybe make you into a bad person. So, I like to think everyone is good deep down at base but, um, it might be that some people by the way they've lived or the way they've been raised are not.

What are my hobbies?

Uh, your hobbies, let's see, photography; um, Art and all that it is; I think photography is part of that; um...going to art exhibits; looking at—buying art books; reading about Art; learning about Art; um, creating art...biking, on a semi-regular basis; um, music, uh...that's all that I can think of right now.

Who are some of my close friends?

By name?

Sure.

Aram, I can never remember his last name, um, Phil, Rich, Sherone, um, Jackie, myself, Roger Smith, I

Doug Wilson

suppose [laughs], it seems that way. Um, you said close friends, uh...I think I'm missing—Jack, uh, Jack [chuckle], um...that's it, those are the major close friends that I can think of.

What are some of my favorite things?
It sounds like a song [chuckle] from *The Sound of Music.* Um, let's see, your favorite things. I think, uh, I know there's a few music CDs that you're particularly fond of, um, are you talking about possessions or...

It's really a broad interpretation.
Your favorite things, OK, so it doesn't have to be a possession of yours; um, the art museum; I think Philadelphia, if you can call that a thing; you seem to like Philadelphia; I think you like New York; um, I'm sure you probably like your camera [laughs]; probably not your hair; certain articles of clothing; I know you've always mentioned, like, your favorite article of clothing...um...I'm trying to think of some food that you really like...but I can't [laughs], but I know there are some that you were particularly fond of, or—I don't know.

Oh, I'd probably have to say that architecture is another hobby, at least an interest, going back to a previous question; um, your bike, I think you like your bike;...uh, Lamborghini; a nice stereo, your stereo which is a nice stereo; your all-utilities-included apartment; um...I guess some of the things you have created like, uh, things that you made with Jack; things that you've made like that—the case to hold certain past memories, I think that's what's in there; the CD case that you made, or CD display case; um, I would imagine anything that you have created, well, that may not be true, may not be your favorite things; um, that's all that I can think of.

What are some of your favorite things?
Let's see...I don't know, things that I like that I have. I like...I like my Subaru all-wheel drive Legacy Brighton station wagon; I like my house, uh, not the way it looks at the time particularly, it needs to be fixed up a lot, but I like my house; um...I like, uh, I don't know, I like my bike; I like—my favorite things— I like the curtains [laughs]; uh, my new redone room upstairs;...my watch: Timex; I like my video camera, it only cost me 65 bucks.

Uh, I mean, I guess I like a lot of my possessions; I picked them out for the most part; favorite things, again, you said it's a broad question. I wouldn't really refer to my family as things but I like my family, they might be one of my favorite things. Um...I like springtime and I like fall, I think I probably like fall better than spring. I like, uh, nice mountain bike trails; I like swimming in the ocean; I like the mountains; I like...um, the sun [laughs], got to give umbrage to the sun; um, is this being dragged on? [Chuckle.] My favorite things...uh, let's see, family get-togethers and reunions...going to baseball games; watching a good movie. I could go on and on. I'll just end there.

Who is the most famous person that you've met?
That I have met, like, uh, like, uh, said "hello" to, been introduced to? The most famous person that I've met? I haven't met anybody famous. I mean not anybody that is a household name—that I've met, not just seen...Maurice Cheeks.

How many people are alive in the world?

Uh, I think there is around six billion.

Are you convinced of God's existence?

No.

Do you think you have free will?

Generally speaking, yes.

How do you deal with that?

How do I deal with having free will? Um, just to realize that you are responsible for your own actions, you know; there are certainly things that are accepted and not accepted by society, things that are legal and illegal but you still have free will to do it if you want to, and, uh, that's your choice; it just has to be a responsible decision, a well-informed decision for whatever you choose to do.

How many ideas of how to live, or what life is about, are your own?

Well, probably none...at least everything that you think...I think, you mean how many, like a percentage or a number? I don't think—I think everything you think about how to live is, um, what you see and observe from how other people live and where they are and what they are doing and if they seem happy and how you're brought up.

Do you remember a time when I wasn't around?

Yeah. I try not to think about it. I'm sorry, I'm breaking down here [laughs].

Can you name 3 very important events in my life?

Oh, three very important events in your life...I have to say that, I mean, I can't imagine that graduating from high school and college would not be a big event anyway. Um, I mean, to me it always seems anti-climatic, but nonetheless, it's a pretty big event. Um, maybe getting laid for the first time....Is that two or is that three? You don't know. Alright, we'll call that two, I can probably think of another one. Um...major events you said, right? So it could be good or bad or anything. I would have to say your parents getting divorced.

What most explains why I am like I am?

I would say that the people that you have met along the way. Um, I think your family has to have influence whether it be assimilating to that or not. I guess I would say going to college and, uh, kind of—maybe finding a group of people that you could really relate to that tended to mold you. Um, so in general I just think it's, you know, interactions with your friends and family, maybe other people.

Do I look different from when you first met me?

Yes.

How so?

Um...well, I guess you look older than when I first met you, because you are about twice as old probably, more than twice as old. Um, I mean, you're talking about physical appearance, look, right?

Yes.

Your hair is much longer, probably your hairline is a little bit changed; uh, I don't remember you wearing glasses when we first started knowing each other; um...I would say your weight proportions are approximately the same, but other than that...

What is the dumbest thing I've done?

[Laughs.] Oh my gosh. The dumbest thing [laughs]. I don't know because you probably don't tell me the dumbest things you've ever done. [Laughs.] The obvious answer is the, um, drive to, I think it's been called now—I call it the Philadelphia Adventure. Do you want me to describe that to the—for the recording here? As a single event, as a single answer to that, I would say driving to Philadelphia when you didn't have your license, and you got lost. But within that are many dumb things [laughs] such as, such as getting onto I-95 by mistake; continuing on, um, and being in the wrong—being in the left-hand lane, not being in the right lane to exit; not turning your lights on when it got dark so you started to swerve and got pulled over by a cop; not having your glasses; not having your license; um, driving—I don't even know where you turned around—driving past the Vet [Veterans Stadium], I know that, which is about a 40 mile drive [laughs]; turning around, passing *all* the exits again, ending up going into New Jersey [laughs]; getting lost in Ewing; getting back on 95; getting off at the Yardley exit, which you thought was the Yardley exit but it was actually the New Hope exit; going into New Hope; getting to a pay phone in New Hope and not knowing how to use the pay phone [laughs]. Sorry to drudge that all up, but I think as an event, from the time you turned onto 95 to the time your mom came to pick you up in New Hope, that period of time was the dumbest period of time in your life [laughs].

Can you name 3 very important events in your life?

Um, yes.

Would you care to?

Oh, OK. Um...well, let's see, now it's me were talking about...getting married; um...graduating, my ultimate graduation, my last graduation I think. And my third most important, no, major event, well, uh, when I learned, when we learned that we were going to be having a baby, which is going to be happening in two weeks. So if you were to ask me this question two weeks from now of course I would say having a child, hopefully. But I could say conceiving, but you don't know when you're conceiving per se, so I'll say finding out, that was a big thing.

What most explains why you are like you are?

Um...you know, the same thing I said about for you, I think, um, my family, my parents, my brothers, my wife, and my friends and, uh—I mean, those are positive influences. I think you can have positive and negative influences: you see things you don't want to be and, uh, you can even have that in the same person as the positive; but, uh, I don't want to be one of those asshole drivers on the road, pardon my French. You know, I like to be generally a pleasant person.

What was the question? [Question repeated.] What makes—oh, OK so, I'm veering off the question here [laughs]; but, uh, when I see someone who is nasty I try not to be that way. So I guess, you know, just interactions with—interactions and observations and relationships.

What would I consider some of my favorite places?

The beach...um...Ocracoke, I think you always used to say that you liked that; um, I'd imagine Philadelphia, I'll say that again, Philadelphia you seem to like a lot; New York; um...I think you like to ski, wherever that may be, say in the mountains; um, I know you like to road bike but I wouldn't say your favorite place is on the road biking, um, that's it. Are you going to ask me what my favorite places...

What are some of your favorite places?

I like being in my house, because it's my house, and it's my home. I like being, um, at my family's places, like my parents' house, and my brothers' houses; I like parks especially parks, like, where you can go biking in or doing some type of recreational activity or having a picnic. I like being on my deck, on any deck, um...I like Chestnut Hill; favorite places...Pollo Rosso restaurant in Chestnut Hill...I forgot, some of these I mentioned before, I don't know what the question was, you know; I like, um, one favorite place I could—it's not a particular place, but a favorite place—a favorite place would be, you know, at a lake house in the mountains with lots of woods around and mountain biking trails would make me—if I had that I think I would be there as much as I could. Uh, that's it.

When was I probably most depressed?

Uh, that's a tough one just because, um, I don't know. I'm not good at noticing. But it never seems like—I mean, I think I may have been able to sense some times when you're depressed but I don't think you talk about it very much. You tend to—I guess when anyone's depressed they tend to probably withdraw. Um...I would have to say, I don't remember this being the case necessarily, but I would guess, and I could kind of maybe sense it a little bit, maybe when you broke up with Sue. I think you were probably depressed then; maybe when you were going through college and didn't really know what, what to pursue or had a change in your—changing your mind, or were in something that you weren't liking that you thought you would like. Like when you were in architecture, and you got out of architecture, but while you were in architecture and not liking it and realizing that you were in something you didn't like, that probably had to be a little bit depressing. Because it's kind of unsettling when all the sudden you find yourself without a real focus.

Um...I'm not exactly sure how old you were when your parents got divorced. I'm not sure—you were probably five or so; I'm not sure, I don't know about if when you're five if you—well, I guess you can get depressed, but I don't know that, I wasn't there. What was the question, "When have I seen you the most depressed?"

When was I probably most depressed?

When were you probably—so I can call for some conjecture. Alright, I will say...we'll I think those things I mentioned.

When was I probably most excited?
I think there's a lot of ties, so I'll pick one. I can think of several things but as far as the most, um...

You can also list several.
I can list several. I've seen you very excited when we've gone skiing. I think you really like skiing...when you've had a chance to go. I've seen you excited, you know, in a car, going to the beach with the stereo on, on a nice day with your friends; um...I think you were excited when you went to Europe, a little bit nervous excitement, but you were definitely excited about that whole adventure. Um...uh...I don't know, I just think in general you seem to be most excited when you're around a lot of your friends and, uh, everyone's having a good time generally, uh, in a very good social situation. One thing I can think of is just when we had that little gathering at Dave and Buster's [nightclub] for your 30th birthday. I think you were pretty excited then just because you had several friends there, probably not everybody that you would have wanted, but several people and I think that, I think you were excited about that.

When were you most depressed?
Um...I'd have to say at different times; um...I was depressed when my sister died. I was more upset than depressed, but I was depressed. But I think I was able to go on with different things relatively OK and—I don't know if I was most depressed at that point. I don't know, maybe I was...yeah, I can't really think of anything.

When were you most excited?
Well, I don't know [chuckle]. These are tough questions. I'd like to say, you know, getting married was exciting but it was also, you know, long anticipated and a busy day. So it was a very exciting time, um, but it—you know, um, that was exciting, that day was exciting, the honeymoon was exciting. Um...I don't know, I think I'm also most excited when I'm out, when I'm with a bunch of friends, good friends, having a good time. I usually get pretty excited, and I still would, I think during—mountain biking really excited me, it was exhilarating excitement. Getting a new house, buying a new house is exciting... and uh, anticipating our, you know, our little baby to be born is very exciting.

What would I consider my greatest achievements?
Going to Europe by yourself I think was a good achievement. I think anyone would consider that a pretty cool achievement, figuring out how to do that, the most economical way possible; getting around in Europe; meeting up with people while you were there and getting back without, at least that I know of, any major disasters. You did a lot better than Chevy Chase did. Um...achievements or accomplishments?

Achievements.
Um, this is what—the question is "What would you think would be some of your greatest achievements?" not what I would think? What do I think some of your greatest achievements...

No, what would I consider...

What would you consider, right. [Exhalation]...I'll say graduating from college, not that, you know, it's we'll leave it at that, graduating from college. [Laughs.] Not that it's a miracle or anything but it's still a great achievement, it's something to be proud of....

Finishing the 5k run, 5k corporate run in Center City a few years ago, a couple years ago, in the manner that you did, looking back on it. I think you would probably consider that a good achievement. Um...you're not going to ask me what my greatest achievements are—you are? Ah, let's see...um...I don't know if this is something you would recognize but I would say, I'm going to say it anyway, that, uh, you know, knowing who your friends are, some of them I know quite well, some of them I don't know as well. But I think a great achievement is, uh, surrounding yourself with the people you have, becoming—having them as friends and them considering you a good friend. I think you would probably consider that to be a good achievement.

And the only other thing I can think of off hand would just be living out on your own, supporting yourself; um, living in your own—according to your own design regardless of what anybody else might say, but just, uh, doing what you like to do, being yourself.

What would I consider my biggest regrets?

Ever telling anybody about the Philadelphia run, the Philadelphia Adventure. Nah, I don't think you really care about that at all. Biggest regret?...I don't know.

What are your greatest achievements?

Um...uh, achieving my educational goals; um, generally achieving my career goals...getting married impregnating my wife [chuckle]. How come you're not laughing out loud, Jim? Um...um...riding back from, riding back on my bike, with you, from Morrisville back to Philly on that windy day and making it up that hill on Susquehanna Avenue. It may go down in history as one of my...although it only took a minute, probably more than that, probably about five minutes—10 minutes, 20 minutes to get up that hill!—um, when my legs were *burning* in pain. I think that was an achievement that day.

What are your biggest regrets?

Uh, I regret, well, my biggest regrets...I don't know, I mean, I guess I regret, looking back on all the mistakes I may have made um, I don't have any major regrets, you know; I have regret sometimes when I feel like I'm not, um, I don't recognize someone's birthday or call them as frequently as I should or invite them over for things or, you know, maintaining relationships. I always regret when I lose touch, when I lose a friend, because of moving away or just a lack of keeping in touch. I always regret that. Um, any, you know—well, yeah. Um...that's about it.

What is some of my favorite music?

Um, since I've known you, I know you like—your favorites have been: The Who, The Go Go's, The Beatles, uh, um, oh, what's the name of that group? Shoot, I can't remember the name of that group. Um, Joe Jackson, I think you liked Michael Jackson. I don't know if you do now, probably not anymore. Um...I think those have been your favorites. George—I know you particularly like, I think I remember you liking George Gershwin but I don't think you would call him one of your favorites, but...um, I wish I could remember that other group. I think it had the word "bones" in it. You know what I'm talking about? I think you've seen them, I think you knew somebody...

Fishbone?
Fishbone! Fishbone. That might be it. Yeah, that is it. OK.

Can you name some of my dreams or goals?
Yes [laughs]. Sort of, maybe. Um, I think you probably dream of being able to live in a house that you would be able to design almost completely and have everything you ever wanted in a house, you know, architecturally, and the way it was decorated and where it was and what it was made of—I think is a dream. What was the other one? Dream or what?

Goals.
Goals. I think it's more of a dream [laughs]. Um, [laughs] let's see, I think I asked you once, I think, about having a family and I think you want to have a family, I think it's a goal. It might be a dream too, I don't know. I think another goal you have is to, um, career-wise would be to get a job that you like to do and paid a lot...wait, I haven't mentioned any goals yet, just dreams [laughs]. But I think you would be perfectly happy, I think, if you had a job doing whatever it was that you wanted to do but as a dream you want it to pay a lot [laughs] because I know there are certain things that you would like to have, um, like a house that you could design and live in [laughs]. Um, I think you would probably would like to, um, you know, become some kind of reco—you know, get some recognition for your projects and art, and maybe even sell it. Sell it? Yeah, well, maybe. You know, but maybe just have it go outside.

What are the most important things one can get out of living?
Um, I don't know, I guess to be happy so that they've lived the life the way they, uh, want and the way they felt comfortable with and to maybe, I guess, think that they, or feel that they, you know, maybe made a difference in the world somehow and that it might carry on after they're gone.

Is working an evil necessity?
No.

Why?
Because...uh, no, I mean working—uh, I don't think it's either. I don't think it's evil or a necessity necessarily. Um, you know, you don't have to work and I don't think it's evil. Just most people need to in order to survive, but that doesn't make it evil. I think, uh, a lot of people get a lot of fulfillment out of working and, uh, in some respects I think it's...some people might think that, even if it wasn't for the money that you need to survive, that there is still a need to work, to feel that you are a working, functioning part of society and, uh, you know, through what you are doing you are somehow...contributing.

Is it hard to be happy in life?
Hard to be happy or to feel happy?

I don't know if there is a difference.
Maybe not...but, uh, I think it just depends on the person; certain things might, some people might—it might be harder for some than for others. I think happiness is a *complete* state of mind. It has nothing to do with what you own or, you know, what you do with your time, what kind of activities that you, you know—I like doing some things, but I don't need to do them just to be happy. Um, I don't know, I guess...I probably wouldn't—I'm sure I would not be as happy as I am now if I wasn't, um, married and expecting a child. That might be hard for some people to achieve, I don't know but, um...but again, I don't know, I think it's just a state of mind. If you feel that...you know, I guess, if you can live with yourself and you like who you are, you should, you know, be happy.

Doug Wilson

In reality, the fact of being is what is most private; existence is the sole thing I
cannot communicate; I can tell about it, but I cannot share my existence.
Solitude thus appears here as the isolation which marks the very event of being.
                                        - Emmanuel Levinas, *Ethics and Infinity*

Solipsism, metaphysical. Literally, "I myself only exist." The
theory that no reality exists other than one's self. The self (mind,
consciousness) constitutes the totality of existence.
                                        - Peter A. Angeles, *Dictionary of Philosophy*

As if any man knew aught of my life,
why even I myself I often think know little or nothing of my real life,
only a few hints, a few diffused faint clews and indirections
I seek for my own use to trace out here.
                                        - Walt Whitman, "When I Read the Book"

www.ingramcontent.com/pod-product-compliance
Lightning Source LLC
Chambersburg PA
CBHW060009210526
45170CB00017B/2122